Table of Contents

BEAR — 4-5
- SHREDDED BEAR SANDWICHES — 4
- BEAR ROAST — 5

DUCK — 6-14
- SOUTHWESTERN FRIED DUCK SALAD — 6
- GERMAN DUCK SANDWICHES — 7
- BBQ DUCK SANDWICHES — 8
- BACON WRAPPED JALAPEÑO DUCK WRAPS — 9
- SUPER DUPER DUCK FRIED RICE — 10
- DEEP FRIED MALLARD — 11
- PHILLY CHEESE DUCK PIZZA — 12
- DUCK EGG ROLLS — 13
- GRILLED TEAL WITH SPINACH DIP — 14

FISH — 15-39
- WALLEYE CHOPPED SALAD — 15
- TERIYAKI SALMON SANDWICHES — 16
- CRAPPIE EGG SANDWICHES — 17
- WALLEYE CAESAR SANDWICHES — 18
- SUNFISH SLIDERS — 19
- WALLEYE PITA SANDWICHES — 20
- TOSTADA FISH TACO STACKS — 21
- WALLEYE STUFFED PORTOBELLO MUSHROOM CAPS — 22
- SALMON SPINACH EEGS BENEDICT — 23
- WALLEYE CAKES WITH DILL SAUCE — 24
- CRAPPIE CHOWDER — 25
- MAPLE GLAZED HONEY SALMON — 26
- HAWAIIAN MANGO WALLEYE — 27
- FLAG UP BAKED NORTHERN PIKE — 28
- JAMAICAN WALLEYE SANDWICHES — 29
- SUNFISH TACOS — 30
- GRANDMA THERESA'S PICKLED NORTHERN — 31
- GREEN CHILIS & CHEESE PERCH — 32
- BEER BATTER WALLEYE — 33
- WALLEYE WILD RICE SOUP — 34
- SWEET WALLEYE WITH BACON — 35
- SHORE LUNCH LIGHT BREADED WALLEYE — 36
- PEPPERED NORTHERN — 37
- FRIED CRAPPIES WITH TARTER SAUCE — 38
- CEDAR BOARD GINGER SALMON — 39

GOOSE — 40-48
- HAWAIIAN SPICY GOOSE BITES — 40
- GREEN CHILI GOOSE STRIPS — 41
- GOOSE FAJITAS — 42
- GOOSE FONDUE — 43
- GOOSE GUMBO — 44
- DEEP FRIED GOOSE STRIPS — 45
- GOOSE NACHOS — 46
- GOOSE & KRAUT BBQ — 47
- BAKED GOOSE WITH SASSY SAUCE — 48

PHEASANT — 49-68
- PHEASANT CEASAR SALAD WRAPS — 49
- PHEASANT STUFFED POTATO SKINS — 50
- SOUTHWESTERN PHEASANT SANDWICHES — 51
- GYROS-PHEASANT STYLE — 52
- PHEASANT SALSA PITAS — 53
- BACON HONEY MUSTARD PHEASANT SANDWICHES — 54
- CRANBERRY WILD RICE PHEASANT — 55
- PHEASANT MARGARITA PIZZA — 56
- CREAM OF MUSHROOM PHEASANT — 57
- COCONUT PHEASANT WITH PLUM SAUCE — 58
- PHEASANT MARSALA — 59
- BUFFALO PHEASANT PIZZA — 60
- MOM'S WHITE PHEASANT CHILI — 61
- SOUTH DAKOTA PHEASANT STIR-FRY — 62
- HONEY TERIYAKI PHEASANT SKEWERS — 63
- PHEASANT ENCHILADAS — 64
- PHEASANT PEPPERONI PASTA — 65
- ASIAN PHEASANT LETTUCE WRAPS — 66
- BAKED BREADED PHEASANT — 67
- PHEASANT PIZZA SHIP DIPS — 68

TURKEY — 69-74
- BLT TURKEY SALAD — 69
- TURKEY SALAD SANDWICHES — 70
- TURKEY SAUSAGE EGG SANDWICHES — 71
- TURKEY MEXICAN RICE — 72
- TURKEY NOODLE SOUP — 73
- BAKED TURKEY — 74

VENISON — 75-105
- GROUND VENISON BOIL BAG OMELETTES — 75
- GRILLED VENISON BRUSCHETTA SALAD — 76
- BLUE ONION VENISON APPETIZER — 77
- VENISON FRENCH DIP SANDWICHES — 78
- H&H CHEESE STUFFED VENISON BURGERS — 79
- VENISON PATTY MELT — 80
- VENISON BURGERS WITH BUFFALO SAUCE — 81
- VENISON MEATBALL HOAGIES — 82
- LIP SMACKIN' CHILI BEAN BURGER — 83
- MITCH'S RIBS — 84
- SLOW COOKED VENISON ROAST — 85
- HONEY MUSTARD MOOSE DELIGHT — 86
- SEARED MOZZARELLA VENISON CHOPS — 87
- VENISON LASAGNA — 88
- VENISON CHILI — 89
- TACO SALAD-VENISON STYLE — 90
- SWEDISH MEATBALLS — 91
- MEATLOAF — 92
- VENISON STIR-FRY — 93
- VENISON STEW — 94
- BLUE CHEESE AND MUSHROOM VENISON LOIN — 95
- VENISON MEXICAN PEPPERS — 96
- VENISON TERIYAKI STIR FRY — 97
- GROUND VENISON STROGANOFF — 98
- CLASSIC VENISON WELLINGTONS — 99
- GROUND VENISON TATER TOT CASSEROLE — 100
- FIRECRACKER VENISON CASSEROLE — 101
- THREE-BEAN BAKED BEANS WITH VENISON — 102
- GRILL BASKET PEPPER VENISON — 103
- VENISON SPAGHETTI CASSEROLE — 104
- CORN RELISH VENISON SOFT TACOS — 105

"For it is by grace you have been saved, through faith—and this not from yourselves, it is the gift of God."
Ephesians 2:8 (NIV)

BEAR *Crockpot / Sandwich*

SHREDDED BEAR SANDWICHES

1 3-4 lb bear roast
1 lb pork roast
1 packet onion soup mix
2 cups water
2 red onions, sliced thin

½ Tbsp black pepper
1 Tbsp brown sugar
8-10 hamburger buns
Bottle of favorite barbecue sauce or Mustard
½ cup of sliced jalapenos (optional)

1. Place the bear and pork in a large crockpot that has been sprayed with non-stick spray or use one of those fancy liners. Next add the soup and water; then add the onions, pepper, and brown sugar.
2. Cook on low heat for 8-10 hours. You should be able to pull the meat apart very easily, if not, let it cook longer.
3. Shred the meat with a fork in the crockpot. Then serve on the buns with your favorite sauce.

YIELD: 6-8 servings

SERVE WITH: Spinach salad and squash.
Have a chocolate shake for dessert.

Ole and Lena went to the Olympics. While sitting on a bench a lady turned to Ole and said, "Are you a pole vaulter?" Ole said, "No, I'm Finnish...and my name isn't Valter."

"How good and pleasant it is when brothers live together in unity!"
Psalms 133:1 (NIV)

BEAR
Roaster / Main Dish

BEAR ROAST

1 bear roast
1 packet – onion soup mix
4 beef bouillon cubes

1. Fill Roaster ¾ full of water or to cover the roast. Add bouillon cubes to water. Pour onion soup mix over roast.
2. Bake at 350° for 5-6 hours.

YIELD: 8 servings

SERVE WITH: Mashed potatoes and gravy, Caesar salad and vanilla pudding for dessert.

Sven and Ole go duck hunting, and Ole is very excited to show off his new hunting dog. They are out in their duck hunting boat, and a couple of ducks fly over. They fire and a duck drops. Ole sends his retriever out to get the duck. The dog jumps out of the boat and runs across the water, picks up the duck, and hops back into the boat. And much to Ole's dismay, Sven doesn't say a word. Another couple of ducks fly over. They shoot and another duck falls. Ole sends his dog out again. The dog again runs across the water, picks up the duck, and runs back and hops into the boat. Still, Sven doesn't say a word. This happens several more times, and finally Ole smugly says, "So Sven, do you notice anything unusual about my new dog?" "Yeah, he can't swim."

"If we confess our sins, He is faithful and just to forgive us our sins and to cleanse us from all unrighteousness."
John 1:9 (NIV)

DUCK *Fry / Salad*

SOUTHWESTERN FRIED DUCK SALAD

6 duck breasts (or 2 goose breasts)
½ red onion julienned
1 red pepper julienned
1 green pepper julienned
1 (15 oz) can black beans drained
1 head lettuce chopped
1 cup of cooked corn
½ of a lime

bottle of southwestern salad dressing
2 eggs beaten
½ cup of milk
1 tsp black pepper
1 tsp cayenne pepper
¾ cup flour
½ tsp garlic salt
vegetable oil to cover pan 1 inch deep

Marinade for duck strips: 1 can Coke, 3 Tbsp soy sauce in a large ziplock bag.

1. Wash the duck well and lay on paper towels for 10 minutes, then place on a cutting board and cut into thin strips. Place the strips into the ziplock bag and then add the marinade ingredients. Marinate overnight.
2. To make the egg wash, combine the eggs and milk in a bowl and mix well. In large ziplock, combine the black and cayenne pepper, the flour and garlic salt and mix well.
3. In a large skillet, heat oil at medium/high heat. Take the duck strips out of marinade and run the strips through the egg wash and then put them into the flour mix and dredge. Then place in the well heated oil and cook until done.
4. In a large salad bowl, combine the lettuce, red onion, red and green pepper, black beans, corn and then squeeze the lime over the top. Add the fried duck over the top and add salad dressing.

YIELD: 6-8 servings

SERVE WITH: Warm croissants with honey will compliment the meal.

Lena tried to give the phone operator her phone number on a long distance call. The operator inquired, "Do you have an area code?" "No," said Lena. "Yust a little sinus trouble."

"All Scripture is God-breathed and is useful for teaching, rebuking, correcting and training in righteousness."
2 Tim 3:16

DUCK *Grill / Sandwich*

GERMAN DUCK SANDWICHES

4 duck breasts washed well
½ cup olive oil
4 Tbsp meat tenderizer
2 tsp black pepper
1 onion thinly sliced

1 Tbsp olive oil
1 14 oz can of sauerkraut
4 hamburger buns
½ cup barbecue sauce

1. Place the duck breasts on 3 paper towels then add another 3 on top. Let sit for 20 minutes.
2. Place the duck breasts in a large ziplock bag and add ½ cup olive oil and shake well. Then add the black pepper and meat tenderizer and shake again and place in refrigerator for 2 hours.
3. Preheat grill to medium/high heat.
4. In a medium sauce pan over medium heat, add 1 Tbsp olive oil, when oil is hot add the onion slices and sauerkraut and cook for 15-20 minutes (until onions are caramelized).
5. Place duck breasts on the grill, and grill each duck breast about 4-5 minutes per side (DO NOT OVER COOK), the middle should be pink.
6. Take each duck breast off, thinly slice and place on the bottom of each bun. Cover with sauerkraut/onion mixture then add barbecue sauce and top of bun.

YIELD: 4 servings

SERVE WITH: Homemade onion rings and coleslaw.

Lena was being interviewed for a job as maid for the very wealthy Mrs. Diamond, who asked her, "Do you have any religious views?" "No," said Lena, "but I've got some nice pictures of Norway."

"For all have sinned and fall short of the glory of God."
Rom 3:23 (NIV)

DUCK *Grill / Sandwich*

BBQ DUCK SANDWICHES (GOOSE)

4 duck breasts, washed well
2 onions, quartered and sliced
½ cup barbecue sauce
½ stick butter
2 cups milk
4 hamburger buns
12 pickle slices

1. Wash duck breasts well then place them into a medium mixing bowl. Add milk, cover with plastic wrap and then place in refrigerator for 2-5 hours.
2. In a medium skillet over medium heat, melt butter and then add onions. Caramelize the onions (cook until brown, do not burn).
3. Preheat grill to medium/high heat. Cook the duck breasts for about 3-4 minutes a side (cook to medium rare).
4. In a medium sauce pan over medium heat, add barbecue sauce.
5. Remove the ducks breasts, cut into small cubes, and then add to barbecue sauce.
6. I recommend buttering the hamburger buns and toasting them on the grill.
7. On each bun, add the barbecue duck mix, caramelized onions and pickles.

YIELD: 4 servings

SERVE WITH: Tater tots and coleslaw.

Ole's boss had been invited to Ole and Lena's for supper. As Lena was setting the table, Ole's boss casually asked Little Ole what was being served for supper. Little Ole said, "I think it is buzzard...because this morning Mama said to Papa, 'If we are going to have that old buzzard for supper, it might as well be tonight.'"

"In all the work you are doing, work the best you can. Work as if you were doing it for the Lord, not for people."
Colossians 3:23 (NIV)

DUCK *Grill / Appetizer*

BACON WRAPPED JALAPEÑO DUCK WRAPS (GOOSE)

4 duck breasts (or 2 goose breasts)
16 pieces of bacon
16 slices of jarred jalapeños
16 water chestnut slices
1 cup favorite barbecue sauce
16 toothpicks

Marinade for duck: 1 can Coke, 2 Tbsp soy sauce in a large ziplock bag.

1. Wash each duck breast then lay them on paper towels 3 thick. Place another 3 paper towels over the top and let sit for 10 minutes.
2. Place each breast on a cutting board and then cut each breast into 4 strips (goose breast's cut into a total of 16 strips). Place the strips in a large ziplock freezer bag and add the marinade, place in and refrigerate over night.
3. Take a strip of duck and put a tooth pick through one end, then poke a jalapeno slice, a water chestnut slice, then poke through the other end of the duck strip. Next, wrap the bacon around the whole wrap, skewering each end of the bacon to each end of the toothpick.
4. Place on a grill at medium/low heat and cook until done. Continuously baste with barbecue sauce.

YIELD: 8-16 servings

This is a great appetizer anywhere, in the field or at home. Most people can't believe that this is duck.

Ole received minor injuries on the job and was taken to the hospital for a check up. Typically, there was much paperwork involved. When filling out the blank asking what number to call in an emergency, Ole put down "911."

"Be still and know that I am God."
Psalm 46:10 (NIV)

DUCK *Skillet / Main Dish*

SUPER DUPER DUCK FRIED RICE (GOOSE)

6 duck breasts (if you use goose, 2 breasts)
3 onions, chopped
6 Tbsp olive oil
1 green pepper, chopped
1 tsp black pepper
2 tsp garlic powder
2 cups cooked white rice

2 Tbsp maple syrup
1 cup peas
1 cup corn
2 tsp minced ginger root
4 Tbsp soy sauce
4 eggs, beaten

1. Wash the duck breasts well and place on a layer of 3 paper towels. Then lay another 3 paper towels on top and let sit for 15 minutes. Next cut meat into very small pieces (the size of a half of a penny).
2. Heat large skillet to medium heat with 3 Tbsp of olive oil. Next add onion, duck, green pepper, black pepper and garlic powder. Cook for 30-40 minutes, stirring often.
3. Place duck mixture in a separate bowl, add the syrup, and stir.
4. Heat the large skillet to medium heat with 2 Tbsp of olive oil, and then add rice. Stir rice constantly for about 10 minutes. Push all of the rice to one side, add the last Tbsp of olive oil and then add eggs. Scramble eggs and then add peas, corn, and minced ginger. Stir all together for 5 minutes and then add duck mixture. Last add the soy sauce, stir well, reduce heat, and let simmer for 5 minutes.

YIELD: 6-8 servings

This can be served as a side dish or as the main dish, either way it's a crowd pleaser.

Ole goes into a lumber yard to buy some 2x4's. "May I help you," asks the salesman. Ole says, "I need some 2x4's." "How long do you want 'em?" asks the salesman. Ole replies, "Oh, for a long time. I'm building a house."

> *"Yet to all who received him, to those who believed in his name, he gave the right to become children of God."*
> John 1:12 (NIV)

DUCK *Fryer / Main Dish*

DEEP FRIED MALLARD

1 picked duck, washed and dried well
2 cups of strawberry jelly
peanut oil

1. Fill your turkey fryer with the proper amount of peanut oil (you may want to try water first then add the duck to make sure it does not come over the top).
2. Heat the oil to 375° and cook the duck according to the weight of your duck (9-12 minutes per pound). Let the duck drain and rest for 8 minutes.
3. In a medium sauce pan over medium heat, add your strawberry jelly and cook for 8 minutes stirring often.
4. Next slice the meat off the duck and place on a plate. Slowly pour the warm strawberry jelly over the top.

YIELD: 8 servings

SERVE WITH: French fries, coleslaw and have a root beer float for dessert.

Ole was wearing 2 jackets while painting, because the directions on the paint can said, "Put on two coats."

> *"Therefore, I urge you, brothers, in view of God's mercy, to offer your bodies as living sacrifices, holy and pleasing to God—this is your spiritual act of worship."*
> Romans 12:1 (NIV)

DUCK *Bake / Main Dish*

PHILLY CHEESE DUCK PIZZA

2 grilled duck breasts, cut into strips
1 small green pepper, julienned
1 small sweet red pepper, julienned
1¾ cups sliced fresh mushrooms
1 small onion, halved and sliced
1½ tsp canola oil
4 garlic cloves, minced
1 prebaked Italian bread shell crust (14 oz)

½ cup pizza sauce
2 oz cream cheese, cubed
2 cups (8 oz) shredded provolone cheese
1 cup shredded or julienned duck breast
⅓ cup pickled pepper rings
¼ cup grated parmesan cheese
½ tsp dried oregano

1. In a large skillet, sauté the peppers, mushrooms and onion in oil until tender. Add garlic, and cook 1 minute longer.
2. Place crust on an ungreased 12 inch pizza pan. Spread pizza sauce over crust and dot with cream cheese. Sprinkle with 1 cup provolone cheese. Top with pepper mixture, duck, pepper rings and remaining provolone cheese. Sprinkle with parmesan cheese and oregano.
3. Bake at 450° for 10-12 minutes or until cheese is melted.

YIELD: 4 servings

SERVE WITH: A hot fudge sundae for dessert.

Ole and Lena were so excited to get a new cellular phone. Ole was to call when he was on his way home from town. Ole called Lena when he entered the freeway, "Lena put supper on, I'm on my way home." Lena says, "Be careful because I hear some nut is driving the wrong way on the freeway." "It's worse than that Lena, where I'm at there are a hundred cars going the wrong way!"

"Peace I leave with you; my peace I give you. I do not give to you as the world gives. Do not let your hearts be troubled and do not be afraid."
John 14:27 (NIV)

DUCK *Skillet / Main Dish*

DUCK EGG ROLLS

1 ½ cup boneless, skinless duck breast, sliced thickly across the grain
1 tsp fresh ginger, minced
2 tsp garlic, minced
2 Tbsp peanut oil
1 cup carrots
¼ cup canned black beans, drained
1 ½ cup cabbage, shredded
8 egg roll wrappers
1 Tbsp cornstarch with 1 Tbsp cold water
Oil for frying

1. Combine sliced duck with next two ingredients and marinate for 30 minutes or longer. Drain duck.
2. Stir-fry duck in hot peanut oil for 45-60 seconds over high heat in a wok or skillet. Transfer to paper towels to cool.
3. Next place duck, cabbage, black beans, carrots, garlic, and ginger in a food processor and mix on medium speed for 2-4 minutes.
4. For each egg roll, lay the wrapper on a flat surface. Place about 2-3 Tbsp of mixture in the center of the wrapper. Fold inside of wrapper to just overlap stuffing. Begin rolling egg roll by starting at the edge nearest you and rolling away from you, like a burrito. When you get to the edge, moisten it with a little of the cornstarch mixture to help it seal.
5. Place egg roll in hot oil, enough to submerse it, and fry until golden brown and crispy. Drain fried rolls on paper towel.
6. Serve with your favorite dipping sauce.

YIELD: 8 servings

SERVE WITH: Fried rice, spicy green beans, and a fortune cookie.

Sven was out shopping in the mall when he met his friend Ole outside the jewelry store. Ole noticed that Sven had a small gift-wrapped box in his hand. "Vhat have you just purchased, Sven?" Ole asks. "Vell, now that you've asked," replies Sven, "It's my Lena's birthday tomorrow, and vhen I asked her this morning vhat she vanted for her birthday, Lena said, "Oh, I dun know, dear, yust give me something with vots of diamonds." "So vhat did you get her?" Ole asks. Sven smirks and says, "I bought her a deck of cards."

> "Consequently, faith comes from hearing the message, and the message is heard through the word of Christ."
> Romans 10:17 (NIV)

DUCK *Grill / Main Dish*

GRILLED TEAL WITH SPINACH DIP

2 picked teal
2 tsp black pepper
½ cup creamy spinach dip

1. Start the grill with medium/low heat. Then place the teal on top and season with black pepper.
2. Cook for about 8-12 minutes then remove and let stand for 4 minutes.
3. Thinly slice the meat onto a plate.
4. With a fork, and dip each bite into the spinach dip.

YIELD: 8 servings

SERVE WITH: Chips and salsa.

Ole was telling Sevn how he had learned to swim as a small boy. "My papa used to take me out in the middle of the lake every day and I had to swim back to shore. Sven said, "Wow that's a tough way to learn to swim." Ole said, "Learning to swim wasn't bad, the tough part was getting out of the sack."

"It is as if the dew of Hermon were falling on Mount Zion. For there the LORD bestows his blessing, even life forevermore."
Psalms 133:3 (NIV)

FISH
Bake / Salad

WALLEYE CHOPPED SALAD

6 walleye fillets cut into chunks
3 cups romaine lettuce, chopped
3 medium tomatoes, chopped
1 can 2 ¼ oz black olives, sliced
10 slices of pepperoni, chopped
3 green onions, chopped

4 slices provolone cheese, chopped
1 6 oz jar of marinated artichoke hearts, drained
½ cup olive oil
½ tsp salt
¼ tsp pepper
2 Tbsp Dijon mustard

1. Place the walleye chunks in a 9x13 glass casserole, drizzle olive oil over the top, and put into a preheated 375° oven and cook for 10-14 minutes (until done). Then set aside and let cool.
2. In a large bowl, combine the lettuce, tomatoes, olives, pepperoni, onions, cheese, and artichoke hearts. Mix well.
3. In a medium glass bowl, combine the olive oil, salt, pepper, and Dijon mustard. Whisk well to make the dressing.
4. Add the fish over the top of the salad and then pour the dressing over the top.

YIELD: 8 servings

SERVE WITH: Steamed broccoli, fresh warm croissants, and for dessert, have a piece of strawberry rhubarb pie.

Ole calls his dog "Carpenter" because he does odd jobs around the house.

"If we confess our sins, he is faithful and just and will forgive us our sins and purify us from all unrighteousness."
1 John 1:9 (NIV)

FISH *Grill / Sandwich*

TERIYAKI SALMON SANDWICHES

4 salmon fillets (8 oz each)
1/3 cup teriyaki sauce
4 hamburger buns
4 pineapple rings
1 Tbsp brown sugar

Spread: 1/2 cup mayonnaise and 1 Tbsp teriyaki sauce; mix together.

1. Combine teriyaki sauce, and brown sugar in a bowl and whisk well. Place salmon fillets on grill over medium heat and baste the salmon with the teriyaki brown sugar mix.
2. Butter the insides of the buns, and right before the salmon is done toast the buns on the grill.
3. In a glass bowl combine the mayonnaise and 1 Tbsp of teriyaki sauce.
4. When salmon is done (about 15 minutes) start making your sandwiches.
5. Start by placing the fillet on the bottom bun, add a pineapple ring, add salmon, and then with a knife spread some of the mayonnaise on the top bun.

YIELD: 4 servings

SERVE WITH: Baked potato, steamed asparagus and a lettuce salad.

Lena decided that she and Ole needed a bit of culture so she purchased tickets to the ballet. That evening after watching the performance for about 30 minutes, Ole leaned over to Lena and whispered in her ear, "I don't see vhy dey dance on their toes. Vhy don't dey yust get taller dancers?"

"Whatever you do, work at it with all your heart, as working for the Lord, not for men."
Colossians 3:23 (NIV)

FISH *Skillet / Sandwich*

CRAPPIE EGG SANDWICHES

8 crappie fillets
1 cup corn meal
1 cup flour in a bowl
3 eggs beaten in a bowl
2 cups peanut oil

4 eggs
1 Tbsp butter
4 croissants, cut in half
4 slices pepper jack cheese

1. Wash the crappie fillets well and dry with paper towels. Place the corn meal in a large ziplock bag.
2. In a medium deep skillet heat the peanut oil to 365°. Take each fillet and dredge in the flour, run the fillet through the egg wash and then place in ziplock bag to coat with cornmeal.
3. Place each fillet into hot oil. Cook each side to a golden brown and then place on a plate with paper towels to drain.
4. In a separate skillet over medium heat, add the butter and then cook each egg over easy.
5. Take the bottom half of the croissant, add two fish fillets, an egg, then a slice of cheese and last, the top of the croissant.

YIELD: 8 servings

SERVE WITH: Fresh fruit, peanut butter toast and a blueberry muffin.

Lena wanted to lose weight. The doctor recommended that she ride a horse every day. The first week, the horse lost 15 lbs.

"The thief comes only to steal and kill and destroy; I have come that they may have life, and have it to the full."
John 10:10 (NIV)

FISH
Broil / Sandwich

WALLEYE CAESAR SANDWICHES

1 egg
¼ cup milk
¼ cup bread crumbs
2 Tbsp all-purpose flour
1 Tbsp grated parmesan cheese

½ tsp dried oregano
¼ tsp garlic powder
¼ tsp salt
4 walleyes (6 oz each)
1 Tbsp butter, melted

Caesar Mayo:
4 tsp grated parmesan cheese
3 Tbsp mayonnaise
1 Tbsp lemon juice
1 Tbsp Worcestershire sauce
¾ tsp garlic powder
½ tsp ground mustard
¼ tsp Tabasco

Sandwiches:
4 hamburger buns, split and toasted
4 lettuce leaves
1 medium tomato, thinly sliced
4 slices sweet onion

1. Place milk in a shallow bowl, add egg and beat. In another shallow bowl, combine the cornmeal, flour, cheese, and seasonings.
2. Wash the walleye well then place on a layer of 3 paper towels. Add another 3 towels over the top and let stand for 10 minutes.
3. Dip fish in milk/egg mixture, then dip into cornmeal mixture. Place on a greased broiler pan. Broil fish for 8-10 minutes or until fish flakes easily with a fork.
4. Combine the mayonnaise ingredients; spread over buns. On bun bottoms, layer the fish, lettuce, tomato, onion, and then add the tops of the buns.

YIELD: 4 servings

SERVE WITH: Sweet potato fries.

Lena stepped up to the clerk in the department store and said, "Can I try on dat dress in da window?" The clerk responded, "We'd really prefer that you try it on in the dressing room."

"It is like precious oil poured on the head, running down on the beard, running down on Aaron's beard, down upon the collar of his robes."
Psalms 133:2 (NIV)

FISH *Skillet / Sandwich*

SUNFISH SLIDERS

16 sunfish fillets
2 cups cornmeal
½ onion chopped
20 oz shredded potatoes
½ cup flour

14 oz favorite coleslaw
4 hamburger buns
2 cups vegetable oil
1 Tbsp olive oil
ziplock bag

1. In a deep medium sized skillet over medium heat add the olive oil, heat for 3-5 minutes and then add the onion and cook until clear. Add the potatoes and cook for 15 minutes, then set aside.
2. Wash the sunfish fillets well. Lay on paper towels then add another layer of paper towels over the top. In a deep medium sized skillet add the vegetable oil and heat to 360°.
3. Put cornmeal and flour into a ziplock bag and mix well.
4. Place 4-6 fillets in the ziplock bag and shake to coat; place in the hot oil and cook until golden brown then place on a plate with paper towels to drain and repeat.
5. Inside hamburger buns layer 1 scoop of potatoes, 4 fish fillets, and a scoop of coleslaw.

YIELD: 8 servings

SERVE WITH: Potato chips, fruit salad, and for dessert a chocolate brownie with a scoop of vanilla ice cream.

Ole stopped into the bait shop to buy some worms. He asked the owner what the cost was for the worms. The owner said "One dollar for all the worms you need." Ole answered, "Give me 2 dollars worth."

> "Do not let this Book of the Law depart from your mouth; meditate on it day and night, so that you may be careful to do everything written in it. Then you will be prosperous and successful."
> Joshua 1:8 (NIV)

FISH *Skillet / Sandwich*

WALLEYE PITA SANDWICHES

4 walleye fillets (6-8 oz each)
2 cups cornmeal
1 tsp black pepper
⅓ cup parmesan cheese
3 eggs beaten in bowl
1 cup flour in a medium bowl

3 cups peanut oil
1 cup shredded lettuce
1 cup sour cream
1 medium tomato, chopped
4 pitas

1. Wash the walleye fillets well and then dry with paper towels. In a large ziplock bag, combine the cornmeal, black pepper, and parmesan cheese.
2. In a medium bowl combine the lettuce, sour cream, and tomato. Mix well.
3. In a deep, large skillet, add the peanut oil and heat to 365°. Next, take each fillet and dredge in the flour, then run through the egg wash, and place in the ziplock bag. Shake to coat evenly, then place in oil, and cook both sides to a golden brown. Place on a plate with paper towels to drain.
4. Take your pita and place a fillet inside, then add a scoop or two of the lettuce mixture.

YIELD: 8 servings

SERVE WITH: Potato salad, green beans, and for dessert strawberry shortcake.

Ole said to Sven, "Why do you suppose they call it GOLF?" Sven responded, "I guess all the other four letter words were taken."

"Trust in the LORD with all your heart and lean not on your own understanding."
Proverbs 3:5 (NIV)

FISH
Skillet / Main Dish

TOSTADA FISH TACO STACKS

20 perch fillets, washed
1 pint of coleslaw
8 medium hard tostada tortilla shells (flat)
1 cup pancake mix

1 cup Italian bread crumbs
2 cups peanut oil
6 eggs
2 cups milk

1. Lay the fillets on a layer of paper towels, then place another layer over the top and dry them good. In a medium bowl, combine the eggs, and milk and scramble well.
2. Place the oil in a large, deep pan over medium-high heat.
3. Combine the pancake mix and bread crumbs in a large ziplock bag and shake well to mix.
4. When oil reaches 360°, take 5 fillets and dip them in the egg wash then put them into the ziplock bag with breadcrumb pancake mix, zip closed, and shake well to cover fillets. Then place in oil until done. Repeat for remaining fillets and place on a plate with paper towels to drain.
5. Now take 4 plates and place 1 tostada shell on each plate. Spoon on a heaping tablespoon of coleslaw and spread evenly. Then add 3-4 pieces of fish, place another shell on top of the fish and repeat one more layer. Repeat for the other 3 plates.

YIELD: 6-8 servings

SERVE WITH: Spanish rice and refried beans. Vanilla pudding for dessert.

Ole accidentally lost 50 cents in the outhouse. He immediately threw in his watch and billfold. He explained, "I'm not going down der yust for 50 cents."

"One night the Lord spoke to Paul in a vision: 'Do not be afraid; keep on speaking, do not be silent.'"
Acts 18:9 (NIV)

FISH
Bake / Main Dish

WALLEYE STUFFED PORTOBELLO MUSHROOM CAPS

2 medium size walleye fillets
6 Portobello mushroom caps
1 Tbsp olive oil
1 tsp minced garlic
¼ cup red bell pepper, chopped

8 oz cream cheese
1 tsp black pepper
1 Tbsp dried parsley flakes
6 slices provolone cheese

1. Preheat oven to 425°. Wash the walleye fillets well and then place in a glass dish; bake until done (12-15 minutes). Set aside to cool.
2. In a medium size bowl, combine the oil, garlic, red bell pepper, cream cheese, black pepper, and parsley flakes. Mix well.
3. With a fork, flake the walleye apart then add to the medium size bowl. Mix well to combine all ingredients.
4. Place the mushroom caps on a cookie sheet then spoon the walleye mix onto each cap (not too much). Add a slice of provolone cheese.
5. Place in oven and cook for 10 minutes.

YIELD: 4-6 servings

SERVE WITH: Your favorite beverage.

Lena was beginning to think that Ole would never ask her to marry him. One evening, as they studied the menu at the new Chinese restaurant, Ole asked "Lena, vould you prefer your rice fried or boiled?" Jumping at the chance, Lena quickly replied, "I vould like my rice thrown, Ole! And da sonner da better!"

> *"Jesus answered, 'I am the way and the truth and the life. No one comes to the Father except through me.'"*
> *John 14:6 (NIV)*

FISH — Skillet / Breakfast

SALMON SPINACH EGGS BENEDICT

4 salmon fillets (8 oz each)
1 cup cooked spinach
4 english muffin halves, toasted
4 eggs
1 Tbsp white vinegar

water to fill bottom of pan 1 inch
hollandaise sauce:
1 stick of butter
3 egg yolks
3 Tbsp lemon juice

1. Grill or bake salmon until done. Flake the salmon in a bowl with a fork and then add the cooked spinach. Keep warm.
2. In a small/medium sauce pan place add all of the sauce ingredients and cook over low/medium heat stirring constantly for 8-10 minutes. When all combined, keep warm.
3. In a medium skillet, add the water and vinegar and heat at medium/high heat. When the water is steaming, add the eggs and then place cover on the skillet. The eggs should be done in 2-3 minutes.
4. Place the English muffin on a plate, add the salmon mixture then the poached egg, and top with the hollandaise sauce.

YIELD: 4 servings

SERVE WITH: Bacon, orange juice, and fruit.

Ole and Lars were on their very first train ride, heading from Hinckley to Minneapolis. They had brought along bananas for lunch. Just as they began to peel them, the train entered a long, dark tunnel. "Have you eaten your banana yet?" Ole asked excitedly. "No," replied Lars. "Vell don't touch it den," Ole exclaimed. "I yust took vun bite and vent blind!"

"Have I not commanded you? Be strong and courageous. Do not be terrified, do not be discouraged, for the LORD your God will be with you wherever you go."
Joshua 1:9 (NIV)

FISH *Skillet / Main Dish*

WALLEYE CAKES WITH DILL SAUCE

1 lb walleye fillets
½ cup white wine
½ cup melted butter
3 green onions chopped
1 Tbsp Worcestershire sauce
½ tsp seasoning salt
1 tsp Dijon mustard
¼ cup red bell pepper, chopped
¼ cup green pepper, chopped
2 eggs, beaten
1 cup Italian bread crumbs (½ will be used to roll cakes in)
1 tsp pepper
Peanut oil (enough to have 2 inches deep in skillet to fry the cakes)

Dill Sauce: 1 ½ cup mayonnaise, 2 Tbsp pickle relish, ¼ cup of chopped fresh dill weed, 1 Tbsp lemon juice, 1 Tbsp ketchup

1. Place walleye fillets in a 9x13 baking dish; pour white wine over top and place in a preheated 375° oven. Cook until done (about 10-12 minutes depending on thickness of fillets), then set aside and let cool.
2. In a large bowl, place the cool fillets and with a fork flake the cooked filets apart. Add the melted butter, green onions, Worcestershire sauce, seasoning salt, Dijon mustard, red and green peppers, 2 beaten eggs, ½ cup Italian bread crumbs, and pepper. Mix well.
3. In a small bowl, combine all ingredients for the dill sauce and mix well
4. In a large deep skillet add the peanut oil (2 inches deep) and heat to 370°.
5. Form fish mixture into small patties and roll in the other ½ cup of Italian bread crumbs. Place in oil and cook for about 6-8 minutes a side (depending on thickness). Serve with dill sauce on top or on the side.

YIELD: 4-6 servings

SERVE WITH: Rice and steamed broccoli.

Ole said to Lars,"I heard that you saved a man's life in a restaurant last week." Lars said, "Ya, I sure did. I advised him not to eat the Lutefisk."

"But the fruit of the Spirit is love, joy, peace, patience, kindness, goodness, and faithfulness."
Galatians 5:22 (NIV)

FISH

Pot / Main Dish

CRAPPIE CHOWDER

20 medium sized crappie fillets
4 Tbsp flour
1 Tbsp olive oil
1 cup frozen corn
2 cups milk
2 ½ cups heavy cream
1 tsp Old Bay Seasoning
2 medium onions, chopped

1 ½ cups white cooking wine
10 small red potatoes cubed ¾ inch
4 cups chicken broth
2 bay leaves
2 Tbsp fresh thyme, chopped
1 tsp black pepper
1 tsp salt

1. In a medium stock pot over medium heat, add the butter, olive oil, and flour. Cook for 5 minutes. Then add the onions and cook until clear. Add white wine and chicken broth; cook for 10 minutes. Then add the potatoes and cook on low heat, covered, for 20 minutes.
2. Add the milk, corn, bay leaves, Old Bay Seasoning, thyme, pepper and salt; cook for 10 minutes, then add the fish.
3. Cook the chowder over medium heat for 15-20 minutes, stirring often. Before serving add cream.

YIELD: 6-8 servings

SERVE WITH: Grilled cheese and a glass of milk.

Lena and Ole and Little Ole were invited to the Swenson's for Christmas. Stuffed roast turkey was on the menu. After dinner, Lena asked Little Ole how he liked the dinner. Little Ole replied, "Vell, da turkey was pretty good, but I vasn't too crasy about da stuff da turkey ate."

"Do not be anxious about anything, but in everything, by prayer and petition, with thanksgiving, present your requests to God."
Philippians 4:6 (NIV)

FISH
Grill / Main Dish

MAPLE GLAZED HONEY SALMON

4 salmon fillets (6-8 oz each)
1 Tbsp maple syrup
4 Tbsp honey
4 Tbsp brown sugar
¼ stick butter, melted
1 Tbsp olive oil

1. Preheat your grill to medium heat.
2. In a medium glass bowl, combine the maple syrup, honey, brown sugar, butter and olive oil. Mix well to make a glaze.
3. Place the salmon on the grill and brush on the glaze, repeat 1-3 times with the glaze. Cook until done, about 12-14 minutes.

YIELD: 4 servings

SERVE WITH: Baked potato, green beans, and a spinach salad.

Ole, who is growing quite elderly, is resting peacefully on his front porch when he sees a cloud of dust up the road. He watches a farmer approaching, with a wagon. "Good afternoon! Where are you headed?" hollers out Ole. "Afternoon. Home to my farm," says Sven. "What do you have in da wagon?" Ole continued. "Manure," said Sven. "Manure, eh? What do you do wit it?" asked Ole. "I spread it over my strawberries," Sven says matter-of-factly. "Vell," says Ole, "ya should come over here for lunch someday. Ve use whipped cream."

> "God made him who had no sin to be sin for us, so that in him we might become the righteousness of God."
> 2 Corinthians 5:21 (NIV)

FISH
Skillet / Main Dish

HAWAIIAN MANGO WALLEYE

2 eggs, beaten
1 cup dry bread crumbs
1 cup flaked coconut
6 walleye fillets (6 oz each)
¼ cup peanut oil
1 medium mango, peeled and cubed
¼ cup white wine or chicken broth

2 Tbsp brown sugar
2 Tbsp minced garlic
1 tsp minced ginger
1 tsp soy sauce
Dash of pepper
¼ cup minced fresh basil
2 cups flour

1. Place flour and eggs in separate shallow bowls. In another shallow bowl, combine bread crumbs and coconut. Dredge fillets in flour, then dip fillets into the beaten egg, then dredge fillets in bread crumb coconut mix.
2. In a medium skillet, over medium heat, add oil. Heat oil to 350°. Fry fish for 4-6 minutes per side.
3. Meanwhile, in a food processor, combine the mangoes, wine, brown sugar, garlic, ginger, soy sauce and pepper; cover and process until blended. Stir in basil. Spoon over fish and serve.

YIELD: 8 servings

SERVE WITH: Steamed rice and carrots. Banana cream pie for dessert.

Minnesota's

worst air disaster occurred earlier today when a Cessna 152, a small two-seater plane, crashed into a Norwegian cemetery here early this morning. Ole and Sven, working as search and rescue workers, have recovered 826 bodies so far, and expect that number to climb as digging continues into the night.

> *"I have been crucified with Christ and I no longer live, but Christ lives in me. The life I live in the body, I live by faith in the Son of God, who loved me and gave himself for me."*
> *Galatians 2:20 (NIV)*

FISH — *Grill / Main Dish*

FLAG UP BAKED NORTHERN PIKE

1 northern pike (2-4 lb)
2 Tbsp garlic salt
2 Tbsp creole seasoning
1 cup fresh creamy butter, melted

1. Take the northern and cut off the head. Next, take a knife and cut open the belly. Remove the guts. Take your thumb and remove the red vein along the center of the cavity. Leave the skin, tail, and fins on.
2. Wash the northern well. Sprinkle the seasonings inside the opened cavity and wrap the whole northern in tin foil (shiny side in).
3. Place either on a grill over medium coals for 10-15 minutes a side, or in a preheated 350° oven for 30 minutes.
4. When the northern is done, open the tin foil, be careful not to burn yourself, and take a fork and peel away the skin. Next, with your fingers, grab the center rib bones, and pull them out while shaking the meat off.

YIELD: 4 servings

SERVE WITH: Wild rice and steamed broccoli.

Lars asked Ole, "Do ya know da difference between a Norvegian and a canoe?" Ole said "No, I don't" Lars explained "A canoe will sometimes tip."

> *"Therefore, if anyone is in Christ, he is a new creation; the old has gone, the new has come!"*
> *2 Corinthians 5:17 (NIV)*

FISH
Grill / Main Dish

JAMAICAN WALLEYE SANDWICHES

2 large walleye fillets, cut in half
3 Tbsp Jamaican Jerk seasoning
4 pineapple rings
¼ cup of olive oil with brush
4 onion hamburger buns
½ cup mayonnaise
2 Tbsp Jamaican Jerk sauce

1. Wash the walleye well and place on paper towels.
2. Preheat grill to medium heat.
3. In a small glass bowl, combine mayonnaise and Jamaican Jerk sauce.
4. Place Jamaican Jerk seasoning in a small bowl. Brush each side of the walleye with olive oil, then dredge each fillet in the Jerk seasoning. Place on grill and cook on each side until done.
5. Place pineapple on the grill at the same time as the walleye and cook on each side.
6. Place the hamburger buns on the grill and toast them lightly.
7. When walleye is done, place walleye, pineapple and jerk sauce between buns and enjoy.

YIELD: 4 servings

SERVE WITH: Sweet potato fries and angel food cake for dessert.

Ole and Lars go ice fishin. Ole pulls out his new thermos and Lars says to him, "Ole, whatcha got der?" Ole says, "Well Lars, dis here's a thermos. It keeps hot tings hot, and it keeps cold tings cold." After awhile, Lars gets curious and says, "Vell Ole, whatcha got in dat der thermos?" Ole says, "Vell Lars, I got a popsicle, and two cups a coffee."

"May the God of hope fill you with all joy and peace as you trust in him, so that you may overflow with hope by the power of the Holy Spirit."
Romans 15:13 (NIV)

FISH
Skillet / Main Dish

SUNFISH TACOS

16 sunfish fillets
1 jalapeño, minced
½ cup sour cream
¼ cup mayonnaise
3 Tbsp chopped cilantro

1 taco seasoning packet
8 small soft tortillas
¼ cup canola oil
½ lime, cut into wedges

Side Items: shredded lettuce, chopped tomatoes, sliced olives, tobacco, and shredded cheese.

1. Wash sunfish fillets well and place them on paper towels then add another layer of paper towels over the top. Let dry for 10 minutes then place in a large ziplock bag. Next add the packet of taco seasoning, and shake well.
2. In a large sauce pan over medium/high heat add the canola oil.
3. In a medium glass bowl, combine the sour cream, mayonnaise, cilantro, and minced jalapeños.
4. When oil is hot, (360°) place the fillets in the oil and cook on each side until done.
5. On each tortilla add sour cream mixture, 4 pieces of fish, a squeeze of lime and other fixings. Enjoy!

YIELD: 4 servings

SERVE WITH: Spanish rice and fried ice cream.

Ole decides he will go into town to buy some groceries. So off he goes. Within a few minutes, he comes to a river. He looks up, down and across, but cannot see either a bridge or a spot to cross. Just as he is about to give up and go home, his good friend Sven arrives on the other side. Ole calls out and asks how to get to the other side. Sven is surprised by the question. He looks up the river and down, then down at his feet and then across at Ole. Sven responds: "You are on da udder side!"

"Jesus said to her, 'I am the resurrection and the life. He who believes in me will live, even though he dies.'" John 11:25

FISH — *Pickled / Main Dish*

GRANDMA THERESA'S PICKLED NORTHERN

8 northern pike fillets cut into 1 inch chunks (bones can stay in)
3-4 cups of salt
2 cups white vinegar
4-6 onions, sliced
1 gallon water

Brine: Boil 1 ½ cup white vinegar, 2 bay leaves, 3 cloves, 2 ½ tsp pickling spice, 1 tsp whole pepper, ½ tsp whole allspice, 2 cups sugar. Let cool then add 1 cup white wine.

1. In a large glass bowl add salt and half of the water and stir well. Add the fish chunks and make sure the salt water is covering all the fish and place in fridge for 48 hours.
2. Drain the salt water from the fish then add white vinegar, enough to cover the fish, and place in fridge for 24 hours.
3. Make the brine and let cool.
4. Place the fish in glass pint size mason jars, alternate fish and onions in layers. Pour brine over top; repeat with other jars.
5. Place lids on jars and keep in refrigerator. Serve in 7 days.

YIELD: 4 servings

SERVE WITH: Crackers and a smile.

Ole and Lena had an argument while they were driving down a country road. After a while they got tired of repeating themselves and neither wanted to back down, so they drove along not saying a word. Then, as they passed a barnyard of mules and pigs, Lena sarcastically asked, "Relatives of yours?" "Yup," Ole replied. "In-laws."

"Because you know that the testing of your faith develops perseverance."
James 1:3 (NIV)

FISH *Bake / Main Dish*

GREEN CHILIS & CHEESE PERCH

10 perch fillets washed well and dried
1 6-8 oz can chopped green chilis
2 cups shredded Colby Jack cheese
Non-stick cooking spray

1. Preheat oven to 350°.
2. Spray a 9x13" deep glass baking dish with non-stick spray.
3. Layer the perch fillets over the bottom. Spoon the green chilis onto the fillets and spread them evenly.
4. Spread the shredded cheese over the entire dish.
5. Bake for 15-18 minutes (until done).

YIELD: 8 servings

SERVE WITH: Spanish rice, chips and salsa, and a large scoop of vanilla ice cream for dessert.

Ole and Sven are at a funeral. Suddenly it occurs to Ole that he doesn't remember the name of the dearly departed. Ole turns to Sven and asks: "Sven, could you remind me again who died?" Sven thinks for a moment and says, "I'm not sure," Sven points at the casket,"...but I think it was de guy in de box."

"Salvation is found in no one else, for there is no other name under heaven given to men by which we must be saved."
Acts 4:12 (NIV)

FISH
Skillet / Main Dish

BEER BATTER WALLEYE

6 walleye fillets
3 quarts peanut oil
1 ½ cup flour
2 tsp salt

3 Tbsp garlic powder
2 tsp black pepper
1 egg beaten
1 12 oz can of cold flat beer

1. Heat oil in a deep large skillet or deep fryer to 365°.
2. Place the fish on a layer of paper towels then place another layer over the top.
3. Combine the flour, salt, garlic powder, and pepper in a medium size bowl. Stir in the eggs, then gradually add the beer and mix well.
4. Dip the fillets in the batter, and place in the hot oil. Fry until golden brown, turning as needed.

YIELD: 4-6 servings

SERVE WITH: French fries, coleslaw, and for dessert have a root beer float.

Ole and Sven wanted to go to Alexandria, Minnesota from Minneapolis, Minnesota, and they chose to travel by hitchhiking. It took them 5 days because, as Ole explained, "I guess we must have used the wrong finger."

"You will keep in perfect peace him whose mind is steadfast, because he trusts in you."
Isa 26:3(NIV)

FISH
Stovetop / Main Dish

WALLEYE WILD RICE SOUP

8 walleye fillets, cut into chunks
1 medium onion, chopped
1 lb cooked bacon, crumbled
1 cup celery, chopped
1 cup carrots, chopped
3 cups cooked wild rice
¾ lb mushrooms, sliced

1 cup flour
6 cups chicken broth
1 tsp dried parsley
2 tsp black pepper
1 tsp mustard powder
2 cups half and half
4 Tbsp olive oil

1. In a large, deep saucepan over medium heat add olive oil, then add onion, carrots, celery, and mushrooms and cook for 5 minutes. Add flour and stir well for another 5 minutes.
2. Add chicken broth and walleye chunks and bring to a boil. Turn to low heat and simmer for 10 minutes.
3. Add rice, parsley, bacon, pepper, and mustard powder; stir and simmer for 10 minutes. Then add the half and half and simmer for another 60 minutes.

YIELD: 6 servings

SERVE WITH: Grilled cheese sandwiches, fish shaped crackers, and for dessert strawberry Jell-O with whipped cream.

Ole walks into work, and both of his ears are all bandaged up. The boss says, "What happened to your ears?" Ole says, "Yesterday I vas ironing a shirt ven da phone rand and I accidentally answersed da iron. " The boss says, "Well, that explains one ear, but what happened to your other ear?" Ole says, "I tried ta call da doctor."

> *"He himself bore our sins in his body on the tree, so that we might die to sins and live for righteousness; by his wounds you have been healed."*
> *1 Peter 2:24 (NIV)*

FISH
Bake / Main Dish

SWEET WALLEYE WITH BACON

4 walleye fillets (6-8 ounces)
8 pieces of thick bacon, cooked—not crisp
1 Tbsp fresh thyme, chopped
Juice of lemon

2 Tbsp Dijon mustard
1 cup honey
1 cup sweet-n-sour sauce

1. Wash the walleye fillets well and dry them with paper towels. Squeeze lemon juice onto the fillets.
2. Brush one side of the fillets with Dijon mustard and sprinkle with thyme.
3. Gently fold the fillets into a bundle, and wrap with 2 pieces of bacon and secure with a toothpick.
4. Place the fish bundles in a 9x13" glass casserole and bake at 425° for 14-18 minutes.
5. In a small saucepan over medium/low heat, add honey and sweet-n-sour sauce; heat for 15 minutes, stirring constantly.
6. When fish is done and before serving, drizzle the sauce over each fillet.

YIELD: 4 servings

SERVE WITH: Steamed asparagus, Caesar salad and cheesecake for dessert.

Ole got back to the farm after a trip to the cities. "Funny thing about the cities. From reading their paper, I found out everyone dies in alphabetical order there."

> *"Then Jesus came to them and said, 'All authority in heaven and on earth has been given to me.'"*
> Matthew 28:18 (NIV)

FISH *Skillet / Main Dish*

SHORE LUNCH LIGHT BREADED WALLEYE

8 walleye fillets, cut into thirds
2 cups dry pancake mix
2 cups dry Italian bread crumbs
1 quart peanut oil
1 ½ cups flour in a bowl
4 eggs, beaten, in a bowl

1. Wash the walleye well and dry with paper towels. Combine the pancake and bread crumbs in a large ziplock bag and shake to mix.
2. In a large deep skillet, heat the peanut oil to 365°. Next take each piece of fish and dredge in the flour, run it through the egg wash, place in the ziplock bag and shake to coat.
3. Add the breaded fillets to hot oil and cook each side to a golden brown. Then place on a plate with paper towels to drain.

YIELD: 6-7 servings

SERVE WITH: Fried potatoes, coleslaw, and for dessert, chocolate pudding.

Ole got notice from the IRS they were going to audit his taxes, so they asked him to bring his records. Ole brought in 6 Beatles and 8 Lawrence Welks.

"In the same way, let your light shine before men, that they may see your good deeds and praise your Father in heaven."
Matthew 5:16 (NIV)

FISH
Skillet / Main Dish

PEPPERED NORTHERN

2 northern fillets, washed well (4 oz each)
3 Tbsp butter
1 ½ cups fresh mushrooms sliced
¼ tsp cayenne pepper
¼ tsp lemon pepper
¼ cup green onion, chopped

1. In a large deep covered skillet over medium heat add butter. When butter has melted add the onion and mushrooms. Cook for 10 minutes.
2. Add the northern. Sprinkle cayenne and lemon pepper evenly over the fish. Cover and cook for 8-12 minutes until done.

YIELD: 4 servings

SERVE WITH: Steamed broccoli, salad wedge, white rice, and for dessert, french silk pie.

Ole and Sven were hunting ducks. At the end of the day, they'd had no luck. Ole turned to Sven and asked, "Do you think we haven't been throwing the dog high enough?"

"'For my thoughts are not your thoughts, neither are your ways my ways,' declares the LORD."
Isaiah 55:8 (NIV)

FISH — *Skillet / Main Dish*

FRIED CRAPPIES WITH TARTAR SAUCE

12 crappie fillets, washed well
1 cup dry pancake mix
1 cup Italian dry bread crumbs
3 cups peanut oil
4 eggs, beaten

tarter sauce
1 cup mayonnaise
1 Tbsp pickle juice
1 Tbsp lemon juice
2 Tbsp ketchup

1. In a large ziplock bag, add pancake mix and bread crumbs. Combine well.
2. In a large deep skillet over medium heat, add peanut oil and heat to 360°.
3. Place the fish fillets on a layer of paper towels with another layer over the top.
4. Take each fillet, run it through the egg wash and then place it in the ziplock bag and shake to coat. Place coated fish in hot oil and fry until golden brown. Place on a plate with paper towels to drain.
5. In a medium bowl, combine the mayonnaise, pickle juice, lemon juice, and ketchup; mix well.
6. Serve each fillet with a scoop of tartar sauce and enjoy.

YIELD: 4 servings

SERVE WITH: Onion rings, coleslaw, and for dessert, a banana split with an extra cherry.

Ole answered the phone one day and came back to the living room crying. "Vell, Ole! Vat in da vorld is da matter?" asked the sympathetic Lena. "I yust had bad news, Lena," Ole replied, "My fadder yust died!" Just then the phone rang again, Ole went to answer it and came back crying again. "Vell, now, Ole, vat is da matter?" asked Lena. "Dat vas my brudder." said Ole. "His fadder yust died too!"

"For we do not have a high priest who is unable to sympathize with our weaknesses, but we have one who has been tempted in every way, just as we are—yet was without sin."
Hebrews 4:15: (NIV)

FISH — Grill / Main Dish

CEDAR BOARD GINGER SALMON

1 8 oz salmon fillet
1 7x12" cedar grilling plank
1 cup Orange Ginger cooking sauce

1. Soak the cedar board in water for 2-4 hours.
2. Wash salmon fillets well, then pat dry.
3. Preheat grill to medium heat. Place the soaked cedar plank on the grill for 5 minutes, then add salmon to the plank, baste the salmon with the orange ginger sauce and cook until done.

YIELD: 2 servings

SERVE WITH: Grilled asparagus, apple and pear salad and cheesecake for dessert.

Ole gives Lena a new cell phone for Christmas. The next day she's at Walmart and the phone rings. Ole is on the phone and asks her how she likes her new cell phone. Lena replies, "Great Ole but how did you know I was at the Walmart?!"

"Being confident of this, that he who began a good work in you will carry it on to completion until the day of Christ Jesus."
Philippians 1:6 (NIV)

GOOSE *Grill / Appetizer*

HAWAIIAN SPICY GOOSE BITES

4 goose breasts
1 small jar sliced jalapeños
1 can pineapple chunks
1 can of Coke
Toothpicks
1 cup sweet-n-sour sauce

1. Wash the goose breasts well then place on a layer of 3 paper towels with another layer of 3 over the top and let sit for 10 minutes.
2. Place the goose breasts on a cutting board and cut into bite-size chunks. Place them in a ziplock bag, add the Coke and refrigerate overnight.
3. Take a toothpick, slide on a chunk of goose, add a jalapeño slice and a chunk of pineapple.
4. Place the goose bites on a medium heat grill. Brush with sweet-n-sour sauce and cook until done.

YIELD: 6 servings

SERVE WITH: A tall beverage of choice served in a carved out pineapple.

Ole explains what happens when you cross a gorilla with a computer: "You get a hairy reasoner."

> "The eyes of the Lord are in every place, keeping watch on the evil and the good."
> Proverbs 15:3 (NIV)

GOOSE *Grill / Main Dish*

GREEN CHILI GOOSE STRIPS (DUCK)

2 goose breasts
1 small can green chilies
1 Tbsp minced garlic

1 8 oz container cream cheese, softened
1 pound bacon
Toothpicks

Marinade: 1 can Coke, 1 Tbsp meat tenderizer, ½ cup soy sauce

1. Wash the goose breasts well and then place on a cutting board. Cut into thin strips and place the strips on a layer of 3 paper towels. Place another layer of 3 paper towels over the top. Let them sit for 15 minutes.
2. Place the strips into a large ziplock bag, add marinade and refrigerate overnight.
3. Combine the cream cheese, green chilies and garlic in a medium size bowl.
4. Take the strips out of marinade. Again place them on a layer of paper towels with another layer over the top for 5 minutes.
5. Take one strip, lay on a cutting board, add a spoonful of the cream cheese mix, and spread evenly over one side of the strip. Next roll the strip into a ball (does get a little messy), toothpick it together, and then wrap a piece of bacon around it and toothpick again. Repeat for all strips.
6. Place each bundle on a preheated grill at medium heat and cook for 5-8 minutes on each side.

YIELD: 10-20 pieces, depending on size of goose.

SERVE WITH: Serve as an appetizer, or serve with wild rice.

Ole complains he never gets a chance to talk at home. He says, "Da only time Lena ever listens to me is vhen I talk in my sleep!"

> "But you will receive power when the Holy Spirit comes on you; and you will be my witnesses in Jerusalem, and in all Judea and Samaria, and to the ends of the earth."
> Acts 1:8 (NIV)

GOOSE *Skillet / Main Dish*

GOOSE FAJITAS

½ cup beef broth
¼ cup lime juice
3 Tbsp olive oil
1 Tbsp garlic
2 Tsp Worcestershire sauce
1 Tsp salt
1 packet savory herb with garlic soup mix, divided
1 tsp Dijon mustard
½ tsp Liquid Smoke, optional
1 goose breast
2 large onions, sliced
1 medium green pepper, sliced
1 medium sweet yellow pepper, sliced
12 flour tortillas (8 in.)
Salsa, shredded cheese, guacamole and sour cream, optional

1. In a large ziplock bag, combine the broth, lime juice, 1 Tbsp oil, garlic, Worcestershire sauce, salt, 1 tsp soup mix, mustard and liquid smoke. Add the goose breast, seal bag, and turn to coat. Refrigerate overnight.
2. In a large bowl, combine onions, green pepper, yellow pepper, remaining oil and soup mix. In a medium skillet over medium heat add the onion pepper mixture and cook for 15 minutes until done and tender.
3. Drain and discard marinade. Grill the goose breast over medium heat until done to your liking —do not over cook (for medium-rare a meat thermometer should read 145 degrees; medium 160°).
4. Thinly slice the goose breast; place goose strips and vegetables on tortillas. Serve with salsa, cheese, guacamole and sour cream if desired.

YIELD: 4-6 servings

SERVE WITH: Spanish rice and refried beans.

Lena said "Der is trouble vit da car, sveetheart. It has water in da carburetor." Ole says, "Water in da carburetor? Dat is ridiculous." Lena states "Ole, I tell you da car has vater in the carburetor." Ole says, "You don't even know vat a carburetor is. I'll check it out. Ver is da car?" Lena says, "In da lake."

> *"And without faith it is impossible to please God, because anyone who comes to him must believe that he exists and that he rewards those who earnestly seek him."*
> *Hebrews 11:6 (NIV)*

GOOSE *Fondue / Main Dish*

GOOSE FONDUE

2 goose breasts and leg meat cut into bite-sized chunks
1 can of Coke
3 Tbsp meat tenderizer
24-32 oz peanut oil (or chicken broth)

Sauces: Sweet-n-Sour, Cucumber Dill, BBQ, Teriyaki, Honey Mustard

1. Place the goose meat chunks into a ziplock bag, then add Coke and meat tenderizer and refrigerate over night.
2. Heat the peanut oil in a fondue pot.
3. Drain the meat and place in a bowl. Put dippling sauces in separate small bowls. Once oil is hot take your fondue forks, add goose meat and cook until done. Enjoy with the sauce of your choice.

YIELD: 4 servings

SERVE WITH: White rice, green beans, and warm rhubarb pie with a scoop of ice cream for dessert.

Ole and Sven, the old retired Norwegian boys, lived at the Old Retired Norwegian Home. One afternoon they were sitting on the front porch looking at the sunset and talking about this and that. Lena, who lived there too, was standing around the corner and heard the boys talking. Being a mischievous lady, Lena decided to play a trick on the boys. Taking off all her clothes, she ran around the corner and raced past Ole and Sven as fast as she could run. Ole and Sven watched in astonishment as Lena runs past. Finally, Ole asks, "Vasn't dat Lena?" Sven replies, "Yah, ay... ay tank so..." Ole says, "But, vat vas she vearing?" Sven shakes his head and says, "Yah, ay don't know, but vatever it vas, it sure needed ironing!"

> *"Now to him who is able to do immeasurably more than all we ask or imagine, according to his power that is at work within us."*
> Ephesian 3:20 (NIV)

GOOSE *Crockpot / Main Dish*

GOOSE GUMBO

2 large goose breasts
16 precooked shrimp, cut in half
4 brats (or spicy sausage), cooked and sliced
2 beef bouillon cubes
4 cups water
¼ cup vegetable oil
¾ cup flour
1 medium onion, chopped
3 ribs celery, chopped

2 green onions, chopped
1 green pepper, chopped
2 (14 oz) cans diced tomatoes
3 cloves garlic
1 tsp dried thyme
½ to 1 tsp Tabasco
2 (10 ¾ oz) cans chicken gumbo soup

1. Wash the goose breasts well and place on paper towels for 10 minutes. Place the goose breasts in a crockpot, add beef bouillon cubes and water. Cook the goose on high for 6 hours. When goose is done, remove, place on cutting board and chop into bite size pieces.
2. Add oil and flour into the drippings. Stir until mixed together. Add onion, bell pepper, garlic, dried thyme, diced tomatoes, celery and Tabasco. Cook on high for 15 minutes.
3. Add chicken gumbo soup, shrimp and sliced sausage to the crockpot along with the goose bite size pieces.
4. Keep crockpot on low and simmer until warm.

YIELD: 4 servings

SERVE WITH: White rice and a banana split for dessert.

Ole and Lars were going ice fishing. It took them three hours just to dig out enough ice to get their boat into the water.

> "Blessed is the man who perseveres under trial, because when he has stood the test, he will receive the crown of life that God has promised to those who love him."
> James 1:12 (NIV)

GOOSE *Skillet / Main Dish*

DEEP FRIED GOOSE STRIPS

2 goose breasts
2 cups bread crumbs
2 cups dry pancake mix
4 eggs, beaten, in a bowl

2 cups BBQ sauce
Peanut oil
1 large ziplock bag

1. Wash the goose well and place on a layer of 3 paper towels and then add another layer of 3 over the top. Let sit for 10 minutes.
2. Cut the breasts in half and then cut into thin strips.
3. Combine the bread crumbs and pancake mix in the ziplock bag and shake well.
4. Heat the peanut oil in a large skillet to 375°.
5. Take each goose strip, dip in egg wash, add to the batter, shake well to coat and then place into the hot oil. Cook until done; repeat.
6. Serve with BBQ sauce for dipping.

YIELD: 8 servings

SERVE WITH: Tator tots, green bean casserole, and for dessert bread pudding.

Ole and Sven went out ice fishing. When they got to the lake Sven sat down on his bucket and started to tie lines. Ole grabbed his hand auger and went out on the ice. Just as Ole was starting to cut a hole, a loud voice said, "There are no fish under the ice." Ole stopped and went another 10 feet and start to cut a hole. A louder voice said, "THERE are no fish under the ice." Ole looked back at Sven, and Sven shrugged his shoulders. Ole took another 5 steps, determined, he started to cut a hole, a stern, loud voice said, "THERE ARE NO FISH UNDER THE ICE!" Ole looked up and said "Is that you God?"
"No, it's the ice rink attendant."

> *"Neither height nor depth, nor anything else in all creation, will be able to separate us from the love of God that is in Christ Jesus our Lord."*
> *Romans 8:39 (NIV)*

GOOSE *Grill & Bake / Main Dish*

GOOSE NACHOS

2 goose breasts
1 can Coke
2 Tbsp meat tenderizer
1 bag favorite tortilla chips
2 cups shredded cheese blend (Colby Jack)

½ cup sour cream
½ cup black olives, sliced
¼ cup green onions, chopped
½ cup favorite salsa
¾ cup shredded lettuce

1. Wash the goose breasts well, place on paper towels, and let stand for 10 minutes. Next, place in a large ziplock bag, add the Coke and tenderizer, and place in refrigerator overnight.
2. Heat grill to medium heat. Place the goose breasts on and cook until done (do not overcook). When done, place on cutting board and let stand for 4 minutes, then cut into small chunks.
3. Take a large pizza pan and cover it with tin foil (helps with clean up). Add the chips, the goose, the cheese then all of the rest of the toppings. Place in a preheated 375° oven and bake until the cheese melts.

YIELD: 4-6 servings

SERVE WITH: Your favorite beverage of choice.

Lena got a job writing headlines for the local paper. After one of the churches in town burned, she came up with this headline: CHURCH BURNS DOWN; HOLY SMOKE.

> *"Let us not give up meeting together, as some are in the habit of doing, but let us encourage one another—and all the more as you see the Day approaching."*
> *Hebrews 10:25 (NIV)*

GOOSE *Crockpot / Main Dish*

GOOSE & KRAUT BBQ

6 goose breasts, cut into chunks
2 onions, chopped
3 cups shredded hashbrowns
2 32 oz jars sauerkraut, juice drained
2 cups barbecue sauce

1. In a large crockpot, combine all of the ingredients. Cook on low for 8-10 hours or on high for 6-8 (depends on your crockpot). Stir every hour.

YIELD: 6 servings

SERVE WITH: Potato salad, a fresh spinach salad, and for dessert, homemade ice cream sundaes.

Ole

always caught his limit and he would never tell anyone his secret. Finally the Game Warden threatened to take away Ole's license unless Ole taught him how he did it. Ole finally agreed to meet him early one morning to go fishing. The Game Warden came with six rods and three tackle boxes, so he'd be ready for anything. Ole showed up with a small brown paper bag. They climbed in a row boat and Ole rowed out to a spot on the lake. Ole then opened his bag and pulled out a stick of dynamite, lit it and tossed it into the water. After an explosion and shower of water, dozens of fish floated to the surface. Ole started to row the boat around picking up fish. The Game Warden was surprised and furious. He shouted, "Ole, you can't do that! It's against the LAW!" Ole calmly reached into his bag and took out another stick of dynamite and lit it. He tossed it to the Game Warden and asked, "Vell, are ya gonna to talk? Or ya gonna fish?"

> "Through these he has given us his very great and precious promises, so that through them you may participate in the divine nature and escape the corruption in the world caused by evil desires."
> 2 Peters 1:4 (NIV)

GOOSE *Bake / Main Dish*

BAKED GOOSE WITH SASSY SAUCE

1 picked goose
¼ cup olive oil
1 apple quartered
½ cup sweet-n-sour sauce
½ cup teriyaki sauce

1. Wash the goose and dry with paper towels inside and out. Next, soak a paper towel with the olive oil and pat the entire bird with olive oil soaked towel.
2. Stuff the bird with the apples.
3. Place the bird in a large roasting pan, cover, and bake at 350° for 15-20 minutes per pound of goose.
4. In a medium glass bowl, combine the 2 sauces and mix well.
5. When goose is done, slice thin and then drizzle the sauce over the meat.

YIELD: 6-7 servings

SERVE WITH: White rice, steamed asparagus, Caesar salad, and for dessert, hot apple pie and a scoop of vanilla ice cream.

Ole got into a lot of trouble recently at the Minneapolis airport. He was walking through the terminal when he spotted his old friend Jack Swanson. Ole made a big mistake when he shouted across the terminal, "HI, JACK."

> "For the word of God is living and active. Sharper than any double-edged sword, it penetrates even to dividing soul and spirit, joints and marrow; it judges the thoughts and attitudes of the heart."
> Hebrews 4:12 (NIV)

PHEASANT *Skillet / Sandwich*

PHEASANT CAESAR SALAD WRAPS

4 pheasant breasts, cooked and sliced thin
2 bags of caesar salad kit
½ cup fresh tomatoes, diced
4 tortilla wraps

4 oz cream cheese, softened
2 Tbsp finely chopped pimientos
1 Tbsp onion, chopped finely
1 ½ tsp chives, chopped

1. Combine the cream cheese, pimientos, onions and chives until mixed together. Set aside.
2. Combine the salad kit with the diced tomatoes. Add the dressing and toss to coat. Lay tortillas on a flat surface. Place ¼ of the cream cheese mixture onto each wrap and spread evenly. Place an equal amount of the salad mixture on top of cream cheese and then add sliced pheasant. Roll the wrap tightly until completely rolled. Slice in half or smaller for a party platter.

YIELD: 4 servings

SERVE WITH: Potato chips and fresh fruit for dessert.

Sven was just pulling his boat up on shore when Ole wandered up with a puzzlement. Ole asks "Sven! What have you been doing?" Sven says "I been fishing, Ole. What a think I bin doing with dese here rods? Ole asks "Did a catch anything?" Sven says (Under his breath: "Dumb svede.") "Of course I catch something. Sven always catches when he fishes." Ole wonders "If I guess how many you catch, will you gimme one of them?" Sven states "If you guess how many I catch I'll give you BOTH a them!" Ole answers, "I guess THREE!" Sven says, "That ain't bad for a Svede. You only missed it by TWO!"

"Let us fix our eyes on Jesus, the author and perfecter of our faith, who for the joy set before him endured the cross, scorning its shame, and sat down at the right hand of the throne of God."
Hebrews 12:2 (NIV)

PHEASANT *Bake / Appetizer*

PHEASANT STUFFED POTATO SKINS

4 large baking potatoes
4 pheasant breasts, cut into chunks
3 Tbsp olive oil
1 tsp garlic salt
¼ tsp black pepper

¼ cup green onions, chopped
2 cups shredded Colby Jack cheese
¼ cup bacon bits
1 cup sour cream
½ cup chives chopped

1. Preheat oven to 375°.
2. Wash the potatoes, wrap in tin foil (shiny side in), and bake for 2 hours. Remove potatoes and let cool. Cut the potatoes in half and spoon out the potato pulp, be careful not cut the skin.
3. In a medium skillet over medium heat, add the olive oil then add the pheasant chunks, salt, and pepper. Cook until done.
4. Take each potato skin and place on a cookie sheet. Add the pheasant, sprinkle chopped green onion, cheese, and bacon bits over all.
5. Place in oven for 8-10 minutes.
6. Before serving, top with sour cream and sprinkle with chives.

YIELD: 4-6 servings

SERVE WITH: Favorite beverage of choice.

Ole was lying back in the hammock and, having just returned from church with Lena, he was feeling a little religious. "God," said Ole, "Ven you made Lena, vy did you make her so nice and round and so pleasant ta hold?" Suddenly a voice from above said, "So you would love her, Ole." "Vell then vy, oh vy," asked Ole, "vy Lord did you make her so stupid?" "So she would love YOU," said God.

> "For I know the plans I have for you," declares the LORD, "plans to prosper you and not to harm you, plans to give you hope and a future."
> Jeremiah 29:11 (NIV)

PHEASANT *Grill / Sandwich*

SOUTHWESTERN PHEASANT SANDWICHES (GROUSE/CHICKEN)

4 pheasant breasts, washed and cleaned
4 large hamburger buns (I like the onion buns)
8 pieces of bacon, cooked crispy
½ cup favorite barbecue sauce
4 pieces pepper jack cheese
16 slices jalapeno peppers (optional)

1. Place pheasant breasts on preheated grill over medium heat and grill approximately 8 per minutes per side or until done.
2. Place 2 pieces of bacon on each pheasant breast and then spoon on the barbecue sauce. Top with slice of cheese.
3. Place each half of the bun (face down) on the grill to toast.
4. Place each pheasant breast between the buns and serve.

YIELD: 4 servings

SERVE WITH: Sweet corn and fruit salad. Sherbet for dessert.

Ole lay dying in his bedroom. He began to revive as he smelled the aroma of fresh lefse wafting through the house. Ole managed to gather his strength and crawled out to the kitchen. Just as he reached for a sample of Lena's lefse she slapped his hand and said, "No Ole, don't you know dat's for da funeral."

"In all your ways acknowledge him, and he will make your paths straight."
Proverbs 3:6 (NIV)

PHEASANT *Grill / Sandwich*

GYROS-PHEASANT STYLE (GROUSE/CHICKEN)

4 pheasant breasts
4 pita bread rounds
1 ½ cup crumbled blue cheese
½ cup sliced pepperoncinis

½ cup pitted kalamata olives, sliced
½ tomato, sliced
1 red onion, sliced thinly
2 cups romaine lettuce, chopped

Marinade: 1 cup balsamic vinaigrette salad dressing, 4 Tbsp lemon juice, 1 Tbsp dried oregano, ½ tsp black pepper, 1 tsp olive oil, 1 Tbsp fresh dill chopped, 1 Tbsp minced garlic.

Cucumber Sauce: 1 peeled cucumber cut in chunks, 1 tsp ground mustard, 1 Tbsp fresh dill, 1 tsp kosher salt, 1 cup nonfat Greek yogurt, ¼ cup sour cream, 2 Tbsp lemon juice.

1. In a large ziplock bag combine the marinade and add pheasant breasts. Marinate for 2-4 hours, then place the pheasant on a preheated medium heat grill for 8-10 minutes per side (throw away the marinade).
2. In a blender, add the cucumber sauce ingredients and puree until all is mixed very well. Pour into a bowl and refrigerate until ready to serve.
3. When pheasant is completely cooked, slice into thin strips. Place the pita rounds in the microwave for 20 seconds to warm up.
4. Make your Gyros with all the ingredients you want; then add sauce.

YIELD: 4 servings

SERVE WITH: Fresh fruit.

Ole and Sven are working on a barn. The wind comes up and blows their ladder over. Ole asks Sven, "How are ve going ta get down?" Sven looks around the roof for a while then says, "Well ders a manure pile on dat side a da barn ve could jump in to soften da landing." Ole said "OK Sven, but you go first, it vas your idea!" So Sven jumps off into the manure. Ole yells down to him, "How deep is it Sven?" Sven yells back, "It's only up to my ankles!" So Ole jumped down to and they both climb out of the manure pile. Ole turns to Sven and said, "Sven vat da hell did you mean it was up ta your ankles? It vas up ta my EARS!"

"I have told you these things, so that in me you may have peace. In this world you will have trouble. But take heart! I have overcome the world."
John 16:33 (NIV)

PHEASANT *Grill / Sandwich*

PHEASANT SALSA PITAS

4 pheasant breasts
8 pita pocket halves

Dry Rub:
1 Tbsp paprika
1 Tbsp ground cumin
1 ½ tsp oregano dried
1 tsp crushed red pepper flakes
1 ½ tsp ground coriander

Salsa:
4 tomatoes, chopped
¼ cup fresh minced parsley
1 small onion, chopped
1 Tbsp olive oil
¼ cup lemon juice
1 tsp coriander
1 tsp Tabasco
1 cup ranch dressing

1. In a medium bowl, combine the salsa ingredients and place in the refrigerator to cool.
2. Preheat grill to medium heat. Combine all the dry rub seasonings then rub on both sides of the pheasant and place on preheated grill for 5-8 minutes per side (until done). Cut the pheasant breasts into thin strips. Fill each pita with pheasant and salsa.

YIELD: 4-6 servings

SERVE WITH: Baked potato and a spinach salad, apple pie for dessert.

Ole decides he will go into town to buy some groceries. So off he goes. Within a few minutes, he comes to a river. He looks up and down and across, but cannot see either a bridge or a spot to cross. Just as he is about to give up and go home, his good friend Sven arrives on the other side. Ole calls out and asks how to get to the other side. Sven is surprised by the question. He looks up the river and down at his feet and then across at Ole. Sven responds: "You are on da udder side!

> "We all, like sheep, have gone astray, each of us has turned to his own way; and the LORD has laid on him the iniquity of us all."
> Isaiah 53:6 (NIV)

PHEASANT *Grill / Sandwich*

BACON HONEY MUSTARD PHEASANT SANDWICHES

4 pheasant breasts, washed well
8 slices cooked bacon
1 cup honey mustard dressing
4 hamburger buns

1. Place the pheasant breasts on a preheated medium heat grill. Cook approximately 8 minutes per side.
2. Butter the inside of each bun and toast the buns on the grill, butter side down, until golden brown.
3. Place each pheasant breast on the bottom of each bun, add some honey mustard and top with bacon, and to top of bun.

YIELD: 4 servings

SERVE WITH: Potato salad and onion rings, for dessert rhubarb pie.

Ole and Sven are standing on a bridge fishing in the river below. Suddenly Sven sees in the distance a funeral procession coming. Sven reels in, turns toward the road, places his fishing pole over his shoulder, and stands at attention until it passes by. Ole says, "Vy Sven, dat vas such a respectful ting to do. I am really proud of you for doing it." Sven says, "Sure Ole, but do ya know I vas married to dat voman for tirty-five years."

"For God so loved the world that he gave his one and only Son, that whoever believes in him shall not perish but have eternal life."
John 3:16

PHEASANT *Bake / Main Dish*

CRANBERRY WILD RICE PHEASANT (GROUSE/CHICKEN)

6 pheasant breasts, pounded flat
1 (10 ¾ oz) can cream of mushroom soup
1 (16 oz) can jellied cranberry sauce
1 (6.2 oz) box long grain instant wild rice

2 cups sliced fresh mushrooms
Dash pepper
Dash salt
Toothpicks

1. Wash and dry pheasant breasts. Pound each pheasant breast flat.
2. Cook wild rice according to directions on box.
3. Heat oven to 350°.
4. Grease 9x13" glass pan.
5. Combine mushroom soup, ⅓ cup cranberry sauce, sliced mushrooms, salt and pepper in a bowl.
6. When rice is done, add 2 Tbsp of cranberry sauce.
7. Stuff each pheasant breast with a scoop of the wild rice mixture, fold over in half, secure with toothpick, and place in glass dish.
8. Place any leftover rice around the pheasant.
9. Spoon the mushroom soup mix over each pheasant breast and on the rice. Place aluminum foil over the glass dish and bake at 350° for 60 minutes or until done.

YIELD: 6 servings

SERVE WITH: Spinach salad, squash and fresh bread, cheese cake for dessert.

Ole goes to the doctor and says, "Everywhere I touch, my finger hurts." The doctor asks, "What do you mean?" So Ole shows him what he means. He touches his knee and says, "OUCH!" Then he touches his chest and says, "OUCH!" Then he touches his shoulder, "OUCH!" The doctor looks at Ole and shakes his head. "Ole you dummy, you got a broken finger!"

> *"So do not fear, for I am with you; do not be dismayed, for I am your God. I will strengthen you and help you; I will uphold you with my righteous right hand."*
> *Isaiah 41:10 (NIV)*

PHEASANT *Bake / Main Dish*

PHEASANT MARGARITA PIZZA (GROUSE/CHICKEN)

1 large prebaked pizza crust
2 pheasant breasts, sliced thin
2 medium Roma tomatoes, sliced thin
½ cup tomato sauce

2 cups shredded mozzarella cheese
8 large fresh basil leaves
2 tsp dried oregano
2 Tbsp olive oil

1. Preheat oven to 375°.
2. In medium skillet over medium heat, add the olive oil, then add the pheasant and cook until done.
3. Place the pizza crust on a baking sheet, then add the tomato sauce and spread evenly. Sprinkle the oregano evenly over the sauce. Next add the basil, placing each leaf evenly over the entire pizza. Repeat with the Roma tomato slices over the basil. Add the pheasant over the pizza and then top with cheese.
4. Place the pizza in the preheated oven. Bake 12-15 minutes or until done.

YIELD: 4 servings

SERVE WITH: Caesar salad. Banana split for dessert.

Ole,

Sven and Lars die in a tragic Lutefisk accident. They are met by God on the stairway to heaven. God says, "There are 3,000 steps to heaven. It's very serious up there. I'll tell you a joke on each 1,000th step you reach. If you laugh you go to hell." So they start walking and reach to the first 1,000th step. God tells a joke, Lars laughs out loud and goes straight to hell. Ole and Sven look at each other nervously. On the 2,000th step, God tells another joke, Sven tries his best but laughs and goes to straight to hell. On the 3,000th step, God tells the last and best joke, Ole doesn't laugh and proceeds to the gate. Suddenly, Ole bursts out laughing hysterically. God asks, "What are you laughing about?" Ole replies, "Oh dat's funny. I yust got da first yoke!"

> *"Therefore go and make disciples of all nations, baptizing them in the name of the Father and of the Son and of the Holy Spirit."*
> *Matt 28:19 (NIV)*

PHEASANT *Crockpot / Main Dish*

CREAM OF MUSHROOM PHEASANT (GROUSE/CHICKEN)

2 pheasants
1 Tbsp olive oil
1 medium onion, sliced
4 cloves garlic, minced
1 (8 oz) container fresh mushrooms, sliced
1 (10 ¾ oz) can cream of mushroom soup
1 (10 ¾ oz) can cream chicken soup
1 (8 oz) container sour cream
1 cup chicken broth
1 tsp lemon pepper
½ tsp salt
1 tsp black pepper

1. Wash and remove all meat from pheasants. Cut into bite size pieces.
2. In large skillet over medium heat, add olive oil. Add onions and cook until clear. Add pheasant and cook until browned.
3. In a large bowl, combine the chicken and mushroom soups and the sour cream.
4. Place everything into the crockpot and cook on high for 4-6 hours or on low for 8-10 hours.

YIELD: 4-6 servings

SERVE WITH: Mashed potatoes and corn along with warm, fresh sourdough bread.

Ole during the Christmas program, kept singing the words, "LEON… LEON…LEON…LEON." The person standing next to him whispered in his ear that he was holding the songbook upside down.

"Though the Lord is supreme, he takes care of those who are humble, but he stays away from the proud."
Psalm 138:6 (NIV)

PHEASANT *Fry / Main Dish*

COCONUT PHEASANT WITH PLUM SAUCE (GROUSE/CHICKEN)

4 pheasant breasts, cut into strips
1 cup shredded coconut
1 cup Italian bread crumbs
1 cup pancake mix
3 eggs, beaten

1 cup milk
Vegetable oil to cover pan 1 inch deep
1 cup plum sauce
1 cup sweet-n-sour sauce

1. Spread the coconut on a large baking sheet and place in a preheated 350° oven. Bake until the coconut starts to brown. Set aside to cool.
2. In a bowl, combine the beaten eggs and milk. Whisk together.
3. In a ziplock bag, combine the bread crumbs, pancake mix, and coconut. Shake and mix well.
4. In a medium skillet, heat oil at medium/high heat.
5. In a medium bowl, combine plum and sweet-n-sour sauce.
6. Take the strips and run them through the egg wash and then put them into the ziplock with the coconut mixture. Shake well.
7. Heat the oil to 375°. Add the strips, turning them as necessary, and cook until done. Repeat with all strips.

YIELD: 4-6 servings

SERVE WITH: Plum sauce. This is a great appetizer and also a main course with homemade french fries.

Ole calls up his doctor and says, "Every morning at 5:00 a.m. I have a B.M." "Fine," said the doctor. "That's very healthy. What seems to be your problem?" "Vell," said Ole, "I don't vake up till six."

"Words kill, words give life; they're either poison or fruit-you choose."
Proverbs 18:21 (NIV)

PHEASANT *Skillet/ Main Dish*

PHEASANT MARSALA (GROUSE/CHICKEN)

8 pheasant breasts
1 medium onion, thinly sliced
8 oz of fresh mushrooms, sliced
½ cup flour
1 cup Marsala wine

1 tsp salt
½ tsp black pepper
1 tsp basil fresh
¼ cup parsley, chopped
3 Tbsp olive oil

1. Wash each pheasant breast well and then pound out each breast flat (I like to use the bottom of a small skillet).
2. Take a large skillet and heat olive oil over medium heat. In a medium sized bowl, combine the flour, black pepper, and salt.
3. Take each pheasant breast and dredge them in the flour mix. Then add each breast to the skillet, cook for about 5 minutes then add the onions and mushrooms. When the pheasant is brown on one side, flip over and cook until brown on the other. Continue stirring the onions and mushrooms.
4. Once the pheasant is brown on both sides, reduce heat to medium/low and add parsley, basil, and Marsala wine. Cover and let this simmer for 10-12 minutes.

YIELD: 6-8 servings

SERVE WITH: Serve over rice with steamed asparagus and fresh sourdough bread.

Ole says the three stages of marriage are like this: First stage, he talks, and she listens. Then she talks, and he listens. The last stage is, they both talk, and the neighbors listen.

"Do to others what you would want them to do to you."
Luke 6:31 (NIV)

PHEASANT *Bake / Main Dish*

BUFFALO PHEASANT PIZZA (GROUSE/CHICKEN)

4 pheasant breasts, cubed
1 Tbsp olive oil
1 tsp garlic salt
1 cup pizza sauce
1 prebaked pizza crust (Boboli Crust)
1 cup Monterey Jack shredded cheese

¼ red onion, thinly sliced
½ stalk celery, diced
¼ cup crumbled blue cheese
½ cup of Franks Red Hot sauce
2 Tbsp ranch salad dressing

1. Pour the olive oil into a medium size skillet over medium heat. Add the pheasant and garlic salt.
2. Preheat oven to 375°. Place the pizza crust on a pizza pan and spread the pizza sauce evenly over the crust. Next, sprinkle the blue cheese evenly over the sauce, add the red onion slices and celery evenly over the blue cheese.
3. Cook pheasant until well browned, then reduce heat and add the Franks Red Hot sauce, stirring well for 3-5 minutes. Then spread the pheasant evenly over the pizza. Add the Monterey Jack cheese and then drizzle the ranch dressing over the top.
4. Place the pizza in preheated oven and cook for 15-20 minutes (done when cheese is bubbling).

YIELD: 4-6 servings

SERVE WITH: Serve this one by itself.

Lena was looking herself over in the full length mirror. Lena said, "Ole, do you tink I'm getting fat?"
"No, Lena," said Ole diplomatically, "you're yust a little fluffy."

> *"And we know that in all things God works for the good of those who love him, who have been called according to his purpose."*
> Romans 8:28 (NIV)

PHEASANT *Crockpot / Main Dish*

MOM'S WHITE PHEASANT CHILI (GROUSE/CHICKEN)

3 (14 oz) cans of white northern beans (or navy)
6 cups of chicken broth
1 Tbsp chicken base
1 Tbsp of olive oil
1 medium onion, chopped
2 Tbsp of minced garlic

1 (7 oz) can green chilies, chopped
2 tsp cumin
1 tsp cayenne pepper
4 pheasant breasts, chunked
1 cup sour cream
2 cups 2% milk

1. In a large skillet over medium heat, add olive oil, then chopped onion. Cook until clear, then add the pheasant. Cook for 10-15 minutes until done.
2. Place the pheasant-onion mixture into a large crockpot. Add all ingredients except the sour cream and milk. Cook on low for 6.5 hours. The last half hour, add the sour cream and milk, then serve.

YIELD: 6-8 servings

SERVE WITH: Grilled cheese and a pickle. Slice of apple pie for dessert.

Ole's neighbor Sven had a boy, Sven Junior, who came home one day and asked, "Papa, I have da biggest feet in da third grade. Is dat becoss I'm Norvegian?" "No," said Sven, "It's because you're NINETEEN."

> "No temptation has seized you except what is common to man. And God is faithful; he will not let you be tempted beyond what you can bear. But when you are tempted, he will also provide a way out so that you can stand up under it."
> 1 Corinthians 10:13 (NIV)

PHEASANT *Skillet / Main Dish*

SOUTH DAKOTA PHEASANT STIR-FRY

2 pheasant breasts
2 eggs
1 large onion, diced
1 Tbsp minced garlic
1 tsp minced jalapeños
1 Tbsp ginger root, minced
1 cup celery, diced
2 cups carrots, chopped

1 cup cauliflower
1 green pepper, cut into strips
3 Tbsp honey
¾ cup sweet-n-sour sauce
3 Tbsp Teriyaki sauce
1 tsp black pepper
4 Tbsp olive oil
2 dashes Tabasco pepper sauce

1. Wash and dry the pheasant breasts. Trim off any fat. Cut into thin strips. In a large skillet or wok, over medium/high heat, start heating the olive oil. Then add the pheasant. After the pheasant has been browned, clear a spot in the center of the pan, crack the two eggs there and scramble them.
2. Add the jalapeños, garlic, ginger root, onion, carrots, celery, broccoli, cauliflower, green and red pepper strips, pepper, Tabasco sauce and teriyaki sauce. Let cook for 20 minutes, stirring occasionally, over medium heat.
3. Add the honey and sweet-n-sour sauce; stir in well. Let simmer for 10 minutes.
4. Serve over cooked rice or noodles.

YIELD: 4 servings

SERVE WITH: Homemade fried rice and a fortune cookie.

Ole was his deathbed and implored his wife Lena, "Lena, ven I'm gone, I vant you to marry Sven Svenson." "Vy Sven Svenson?" his wife asked. "You've hated him all of your life!" Stil do, "gasped Ole.

"Finally, brothers, whatever is true, whatever is noble, whatever is right, whatever is pure, whatever is lovely, whatever is admirable—if anything is excellent or praiseworthy—think about such things."
Philippian 4:8 (NIV)

PHEASANT *Grill / Appetizer*

HONEY TERIYAKI PHEASANT SKEWERS (GROUSE/CHICKEN)

4 pheasant breasts
2 cups honey
2 cups teriyaki sauce
1 tsp minced garlic

1 dash Tabasco
¼ cup sesame seeds
12-14 medium wooden skewers (soaked in water for 1 hour before using)

1. Cut each pheasant breast into 4 long strips.
2. In a medium bowl, combine honey, Teriyaki sauce, garlic and Tabasco.
3. Preheat grill to medium/low heat.
4. Sew each pheasant strip onto a skewer, then place on the grill. Brush each skewer with the honey-teriyaki mix on each side and then sprinkle the sesame seed onto each skewer.
5. Cook until done (try not to overcook).

YIELD: 4-6 servings

SERVE WITH: White rice, and for dessert, chocolate pudding.

Lena had just been awarded a divorce. She had charged non-support. The judge said to Ole, "I have decided to give your wife $400 a month for support." "Well, dat's fine, Judge," said Ole. "And once in a while, I'll try to chip in a few bucks myself."

"But seek first his kingdom and his righteousness, and all these things will be given to you as well."
Matthew 6:33 (NIV)

PHEASANT *Bake / Main Dish*

PHEASANT ENCHILADAS (GROUSE/CHICKEN)

4 pheasant breasts, cooked and chopped
1 (8 oz) package cream cheese
2 tsp onion powder
¼ tsp pepper
2 cans cream of chicken soup

2 (10 oz) cans diced tomatoes
2 (10 oz) cans diced green chilies
8 flour tortillas, burrito style
2 cups shredded cheddar cheese
Jalapeño slices, optional

1. Preheat oven to 350°.
2. Mix cream cheese, onion powder, pepper, cream of chicken soup, tomatoes, green chilies and sour cream; divide into 2 separate bowls. Add chopped pheasant into one of the bowls.
3. Place 1/3 cup of pheasant mixture down the center of each tortilla, then roll and place in a 9x13 greased baking dish, placing rolled side down. Repeat.
4. Spoon the remaining soup mixture over the tortillas and bake uncovered for 30 minutes.
5. Sprinkle the shredded cheese on top and bake an additional 5 minutes or until cheese is melted.

YIELD: 4-6 servings

SERVE WITH: Spanish rice and refried beans, for dessert, strawberry shortcake.

Ole was on an airplane trip. His seat partner was a gorgeous young woman who made Ole's heart skip a beat. "Where are you going?" asked the young woman. "Minneapolis," answered Ole. "Same here," said the gal. "I'm going to Minneapolis to meet the man of my dreams…because I read in a magazine that the most romantic men in the world are Norwegians and American Indians. By the way, what is your name?" Ole said shyly, "Ole Red Feather."

"Therefore, if anyone is in Christ, he is a new creation; the old has gone, the new has come!"
2 Corinthians 5:17 (NIV)

PHEASANT *Bake / Main Dish*

PHEASANT PEPPERONI PASTA (GROUSE/CHICKEN)

2 lbs uncooked rotini spiral pasta noodles
1 (45 oz) jar spaghetti sauce
3 cups sliced mushrooms
6 pheasant breasts, diced into chunks
1 large onion, chopped
2 Tbsp fresh basil, chopped
1 Tbsp minced garlic

2 cups shredded mozzarella cheese
2 cups shredded cheddar cheese
25 pepperoni slices
2 Tbsp pesto
2 Tbsp olive oil
1 Tbsp dried oregano
1 9x13" deep disposable pan (lasagna type pan)

1. Preheat oven to 350°.
2. In a large pot with boiling water, cook pasta until done.
3. In a large deep skillet over medium heat, add olive oil, then add onion, garlic, pheasant, basil, pesto, oregano and mushrooms. Cook until pheasant is done and onions are clear. Add the spaghetti sauce and cook over medium/low heat for 15 minutes.
4. Spray the 9x13" pan with nonstick spray. Add the pasta, then stir in the sauce mixture. Mix well.
5. Cover the top with mozzarella and cheddar cheese, then add the pepperoni slices over the entire top. Bake, uncovered, approximately 15-20 minutes until cheese is melted.

YIELD: 4-6 servings

SERVE WITH: Baked potato, creamed corn and spinach salad. Tiramisu for dessert.

The doctor tells Ole he only has a few days left to live. Ole thinks a little, looks hard at Lena, and says, "Lena, promise me, swear to me, that when I'm gone, you'll marry Sven Svenson."
"SVEN SVENSON???" she shrieks. "You've hated him all your life!" Ole answers, "Yep, I still do."

"Therefore, as God's chosen people, holy and dearly loved, clothe yourselves with compassion, kindness, humility, gentleness and patience."
Colossians 3:12 (NIV)

PHEASANT *Skillet / Main Dish*

ASIAN PHEASANT LETTUCE WRAPS

3 Tbsp hoisin sauce
1 Tbsp rice vinegar
1 Tbsp soy sauce
1 ½ tsp brown sugar
1/3 tsp hot chili sauce
1 ¾ tsp sesame oil, divided
1 Tbsp olive oil
3 green onions, chopped

1 tsp minced garlic
½ tsp ground ginger
½ red bell pepper, chopped
8 oz mushrooms, chopped
4 pheasant breasts, sliced
1 head of iceberg lettuce, cored and rinsed
(or 8 lettuce leaves)

1. In a small bowl, stir together hoisin sauce, vinegar, soy sauce, brown sugar, chili sauce, and ¼ tsp sesame oil. Set aside.
2. Heat olive oil and 1 ½ teaspoons sesame oil in a skillet over medium/high heat. Add pheasant and heat thoroughly. Add green onions, garlic, and ginger. Cook for 2 minutes. Add red bell pepper and mushrooms; cook for 2 minutes. Add the sauce mixture to the skillet, tossing to coat.
3. Spoon the pheasant mixture into the lettuce leaves.

YIELD: 4 servings

SERVE WITH: Egg rolls, fried rice and a fortune cookie.

Ole bought Lena a piano for her birthday. A few weeks later, Lars inquired how she was doing with it. "Oh," said Ole, "I persvaded her to switch to a clarinet." "How come?" asked Lars. "Vell," Ole answered, "because vith a clarinet, she can't sing."

> *"Therefore, since we are surrounded by such a great cloud of witnesses, let us throw off everything that hinders and the sin that so easily entangles, and let us run with perseverance the race marked out for us."*
> Hebrews 12:1 (NIV)

PHEASANT *Bake / Main Dish*

BAKED BREADED PHEASANT

4-6 pheasant breasts
2 cups buttermilk
Olive oil
1 ½ cups bread crumbs

3 Tbsp of chopped dehydrated onion
¼ tsp garlic salt
½ tsp black ground pepper

1. Place pheasant breasts in a shallow dish and pour buttermilk over to cover. Refrigerate for 1-4 hours.
2. Preheat oven to 375°. Prepare a baking sheet with a thin layer of olive oil.
3. In a shallow dish, combine bread crumbs, dehydrated onion, garlic salt and pepper. Remove pheasant from the buttermilk, allowing excess buttermilk to drip off, dredge in the bread crumb mixture. Firmly press the bread crumbs into the pheasant on both sides to generously coat. Shake excess coating off and transfer to the baking sheet.
4. Drizzle the top of each pheasant breast with oil. Bake for 15-20 minutes or until pheasant is firm and cooked through.

YIELD: 4 servings

SERVE WITH: Baked potato and creamed corn.
Have a strawberry milkshake for dessert.

Ole and Lena own a cafe. Their sign says "Please don't criticize da coffee, someday you may be old und veak too!"

67

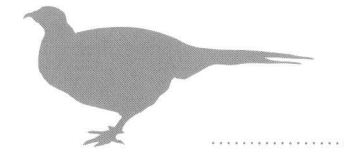

"Jesus replied: 'Love the Lord your God with all your heart and with all your soul and with all your mind.'"
Matthew 22:37 (NIV)

PHEASANT *Skillet / Main Dish*

PHEASANT PIZZA SHIP DIPS

1 frozen white bread loaf
2 pheasant breasts, cut into bite size chunks
¼ onion, chopped
¼ cup green olives, chopped

2 cups shredded Colby Jack cheese
2 cups favorite spaghetti sauce
2 Tbsp olive oil

1. Put frozen bread loaf on a greased cookie sheet. Cover loaf with a paper towel. Let rise at room temperature for 6-8 hours.
2. In a medium skillet over medium heat, heat olive oil and let heat for 3-5 minutes. Add onion and cook until clear, then add pheasant chunks and cook for 10-15 minutes until fully cooked.
3. With greased fingers, shape the dough into a 9x13 size on the greased cookie sheet. Put pizza toppings in the middle of the dough. Fold the dough towards the center and pinch together until sealed.
4. Bake at 350° for 20 minutes in oven, then let cool and cut into slices. Serve with warm spaghetti sauce.

YIELD: 8 servings

SERVE WITH: Caesar salad and mozzarella sticks. Vanilla pudding for dessert.

Sven
Says, "Ole, stand in front of my truck and tell me if my blinkers are working." Ole, " Yes…no…yes…no…yes…no…yes…no."

> *"Keep your lives free from the love of money and be content with what you have, because God has said, 'Never will I leave you; never will I forsake you.'"*
> *Hebrews 13:5 (NIV)*

TURKEY *Salad*

BLT TURKEY SALAD (GROUSE/CHICKEN/PHEASANT)

1 tsp black pepper
6 cups torn romaine or leaf lettuce
4 cups cubed cooked turkey
1 ½ cups chopped tomatoes
1 ½ cups (6 oz) shredded cheddar cheese
10 bacon strips, cooked and crumbled
½ cup chopped green pepper
½ cup chopped red onion
½ cup chopped cucumber

Dressing:
1 cup (8 oz) plain yogurt
1 cup mayonnaise
¼ cup sugar
¼ cup red wine vinegar
1 tsp garlic powder
1 tsp dry mustard

1. In a large salad bowl, combine the first nine ingredients. Just before serving, whisk together the dressing ingredients. Pour over the turkey mixture. Toss to coat.

YIELD: 4 servings

SERVE WITH: French bread, for dessert, vanilla ice cream.

Ole and Lena visit New York City. Caught in traffic on East 46th, a homeless person starts washing the windshield. Ole rolls down the window. "Eh, how's it going?" the homeless guy says. "Ohhh it's OK." Ole says. "Hey, where are you folks from?" said the homeless guy, "Ohh ve're from Minnesota." said Ole. "Ohhh Minnesota, I've been there. I met the ugliest woman I ever saw in Minnesota!" the homeless guys says. Lena asks "Vat's he saying Ole?" Ole says "Ohhh he says he knows you, Lena."

"But he said to me, My grace is sufficient for you, for my power is made perfect in weakness. Therefore I will boast all the more gladly about my weaknesses, so that Christ's power may rest on me."
2 Corinthians 12:9 (NIV)

TURKEY *Main Dish*

TURKEY SALAD SANDWICHES (GROUSE/CHICKEN/PHEASANT)

1½ cups cubed cooked turkey breast
¼ cup thinly sliced celery
½ cups grapes
3 Tbsp chopped cashews
1 green onion, chopped
¼ cup reduced-fat mayonnaise

2 Tbsp reduced-fat plain yogurt
¼ tsp salt
¼ tsp garlic powder
¼ tsp pepper
4 lettuce leaves
4 tortilla wraps

1. In a small bowl, combine the turkey, celery, cashews, and onion. Combine the mayonnaise, yogurt, salt and pepper in a separate bowl. Then add the mayonnaise mixture to turkey mixture and stir to coat.
2. Place a lettuce leaf on each tortilla, then top with ½ cup of turkey salad.

YIELD: 4 servings

SERVE WITH: Potato chips and a pickle spear. Chocolate chip cookies for dessert.

Sven and Ole were working for the city of Minneapolis. Sven would dig a hole - he would dig, dig, dig. Ole would come along and fill the hole - fill, fill, fill. Sven and Ole worked furiously; one digging a hole, the other filling it up again. A man was watching from the sidewalk and couldn't believe how hard these men were working, but couldn't understand what they were doing. Finally he had to ask them. He said to Sven, the hole digger, "I appreciate how hard you work, but what are you doing? You dig a hole and your partner comes along behind you and fills it up again!" Sven, hole digger, replied, "Yeah, I suppose it does look funny, but Lars, da guy who plants da trees is sick today."

"For God did not give us a spirit of timidity, but a spirit of power, of love and of self-discipline."
2 Timothy 1:7 (NIV)

TURKEY *Skillet / Main Dish*

TURKEY SAUSAGE EGG SANDWICHES

¼ cup grated parmesan cheese
3 Tbsp minced fresh parsley
2 Tbsp fresh sage
2 garlic cloves, minced
½ tsp salt
½ tsp black pepper

1½ lbs lean ground turkey
1 Tbsp olive oil
6 eggs
12 pieces of toast
6 slices of American cheese

1. In a large bowl, combine the first six ingredients. Crumble turkey over mixture and mix well. Shape into twelve 3" patties.
2. In a large skillet coated with nonstick cooking spray, cook patties in oil in batches over medium heat for 3-5 minutes on each side or until the meat is no longer pink. Drain on paper towels if necessary.
3. In a large skillet, coated with nonstick spray, over medium heat, cook the 6 eggs to over medium. Next stack the sandwiches with a turkey patty on a slice of toast, add a slice of cheese, an egg, the 2nd half of toast and repeat.

YIELD: 6 servings

SERVE WITH: Hash brown patties and fresh fruit.

Ole and Sven went fishing one day in a rented boat and were catching fish like crazy. Ole said, "We better mark dis spot so ve can come back tomorrow and catch more fish." Sven then proceeded to mark the bottom of the boat with a large 'X'. Ole asked him what he was doing, and Sven told him he was marking the spot so they could come back to catch more fish. Ole said, " Ya big dummy, how do ya know ve are going ta get da same boat tomorrow?"

"For we are God's workmanship, created in Christ Jesus to do good works, which God prepared in advance for us to do."
Ephesians 2:10 (NIV)

TURKEY *Skillet / Main Dish*

TURKEY MEXICAN RICE (GROUSE/CHICKEN/PHEASANT)

1 lb turkey breast, cut into 1-inch chunks
1 onion, chopped
2 cups cooked brown or white rice
2 Tbsp olive oil
1 Tbsp minced garlic
1 (15 oz) can black beans, drained
1 cup corn, cooked
1 red pepper, chopped
1 (16 oz) jar of taco sauce
½ cup fresh cilantro, chopped fine
3 eggs, beaten

1. In a large skillet, over medium heat, add 1 Tbsp of olive oil and the egg. Scramble, then place in a separate bowl and set aside.
2. In the same skillet over medium heat, add 1 Tbsp of olive oil and then add the turkey chunks, onion, red pepper, and garlic. Cook until turkey is done, approximately 8-10 minutes.
3. Add the beans, rice, corn, and taco sauce. Mix well and cook for another 5 minutes. Add eggs and cilantro; mix well and simmer for 8-10 minutes.

YIELD: 6 servings

SERVE WITH: Serve as a side dish or main course.

Ole went to the doctor because he was feeling a little sick. After a few tests the doctor told Ole, "I'm sorry to tell you that you have a rare disease that is incurable and you are going to die in 6 months. But to help you out I'm going to prescribe that you move in with your mother-in-law." Ole replied, "Criminy, dat's bad Doc, but vy should I move in vit my old mudder-in-law." The Doc said, "Because that will be the longest 6 months of your life."

> *"This is how we know what love is: Jesus Christ laid down his life for us. And we ought to lay down our lives for our brothers."*
> *1 John 3:16 (NIV)*

TURKEY *Dutch Oven / Main Dish*

TURKEY NOODLE SOUP

3 (14 ½ oz) cans of chicken broth
¼ cup celery, chopped
¼ cup carrot, chopped
1 Tbsp onion, minced
1 Tbsp parsley, minced

⅛ tsp bay leaves, chopped
2 cups diced cooked turkey
1 package egg noodles
   (or your favorite soup noodles)

1. In a 3-quart Dutch oven over medium heat, combine all ingredients except the turkey and noodles. Cover and heat to boiling. Reduce heat to low. Cook 20 minutes until vegetables are tender, stirring occasionally.
2. Cook noodles according to package.
3. Add turkey and cooked noodles. Heat through.

YIELD: 4-6 servings

SERVE WITH: Grilled cheese and saltine crackers. Oatmeal cookies for dessert.

Lena competed with a French woman and an English woman in the breast stroke division of an English Channel swim competition. The French woman came in first, the English woman second. Lena reached the shore completely exhausted. She remarked, "I don't vant to complain, but I tink dose utter two girls used der arms."

"For God did not send his Son into the world to condemn the world, but to save the world through him."
John 3:17 (NIV)

TURKEY *Bake / Main Dish*

BAKED TURKEY

1 whole 12 lb turkey
¼ cup olive oil
¼ cup rosemary
2 oranges, cut in half
1 apple, quartered
1 large oven cooking bag

1. Wash the turkey well and take out the giblets. Pat the turkey very well with paper towels and then place on a cutting board. Take another paper towel and soak it with some of the olive oil, pat the turkey well all over. Sprinkle rosemary over the entire bird.
2. Stuff the bird with the oranges and apple.
3. Place the bird in the oven bag, then into a large roasting pan. Bake in a preheated 350° oven for 3 to 3 ½ hours (if bird weighs more add more time–you want the meat in the thigh to be 180°).

YIELD: 6-8 servings

SERVE WITH: Mashed potatoes, cranberries, green bean casserole and for dessert, pumpkin pie.

Ole ran a dairy farm and did pretty well. He adopted a slogan which hung on the barn wall, "All that I am … I owe to udders."

> *"Greater love has no one than this, that he lay down his life for his friends."*
> John 15:13 (NIV)

VENISON *Skillet / Breakfast*

GROUND VENISON BOIL BAG OMELETTES

¾ lb ground venison
8 eggs
½ cup chopped yellow onion
½ cup chopped green pepper

1 cup shredded cheese
1 tsp black pepper
1 tsp dried oregano
4 quart size freezer ziplock bags

1. In a medium skillet over medium heat, add the ground venison. Season with the black pepper and oregano and cook until done. Set aside to cool.
2. In a large pot, fill the pot 1/3 full of water and bring to a boil.
3. Crack 2 eggs into each ziplock. Then divide the venison, onion, pepper, and cheese equally into the bags.
4. Seal each bag, squish the bags well and then open and let all air out. Seal bag again and place in the boiling water. Cook for approximately 20 minutes.
5. Remove bags from water (careful—hot). Open each bag, and place on a plate, then serve.

YIELD: 4 servings

SERVE WITH: Bacon, fresh fruit, and blueberry muffins.

Sven and Ole bought a new car. They were so excited about it that when they got home they locked the keys in the car. Sven says to Ole, "I thought you had the keys." Ole says, "You ver driving, da driver always takes da keys." "Well," says Sven, "It doesn't much matter, da question is vat are ve going ta do about it." Ole says, "I don't know, but ve bedder come up vit someting fast because it looks like rain, and you had ta go and leave da top down."

> "Then God said, 'Let us make man in our image, in our likeness, and let them rule over the fish of the sea and the birds of the air, over the livestock, over all the earth, and over all the creatures that move along the ground.'"
> Genesis 1:26 (NIV)

VENISON *Grill / Salad*

GRILLED VENISON BRUSCHETTA SALAD

1 ½ lbs venison tenderloin steaks (1 in. thick)
½ tsp salt
¼ tsp pepper
6 slices Italian bread (½ in. thick)
3 cups fresh baby spinach

½ red pepper sliced
½ yellow pepper sliced
Crumbled blue cheese, optional
¾ cup blue cheese salad dressing

1. Sprinkle steaks with salt and pepper. Grill, covered, over medium heat for 6-8 minutes on each side or until meat reaches desired doneness (for medium-rare, a meat thermometer should read 145°; medium, 160°; well done, 170°). Let stand for 5 minutes.
2. Grill bread, covered, for 1-2 minutes on each side or until toasted. Place on salad plates.
3. Thinly slice steak; arrange over toast. Top with spinach and red and yellow peppers. Sprinkle with cheese if desired. Drizzle with dressing.

YIELD: 2-4 servings

SERVE WITH: A slice of warm pumpkin pie.

Ole and Lena were fast asleep when all of a sudden the phone rings. Ole wakens and goes to answer it. "How the heck should I know, that's a thousand miles away!!" he barks into the phone and then slams down the receiver. "Who was that?" asks Lena. "I have no idea, Lena, " answers Ole. "Somebody wanted to know if the coast is clear."

"But in your hearts set apart Christ as Lord. Always be prepared to give an answer to everyone who asks you to give the reason for the hope that you have. But do this with gentleness and respect."
1 Peter 3:15 (NIV)

VENISON *Grill / Appetizer*

BLUE ONION VENISON APPETIZER

2 lb venison loin
3 onions, sliced
2 Tbsp minced garlic
6 Tbsp olive oil
1 Tbsp black pepper
1 gallon size ziplock bag

10 pieces of baguette bread, cut ¼ inch thick
8 oz cream cheese
½ cup crumbled blue cheese
¼ tsp garlic salt
1 dash Tabasco

1. Preheat grill to medium heat.
2. Preheat oven to 375°.
3. Wash the venison loin well and place on a layer of 3 paper towels. Place another layer of 3 paper towels over the top of the loin and let stand for ten minutes. Place the loin in a gallon size ziplock bag, add 3 Tbsp of olive oil, zip shut and shake. Open, add the black pepper, then zip shut and shake again and let stand at room temperature for 10 or more minutes.
4. In a medium sauce pan over medium/low heat, add olive oil and then add onions. Cook until caramelized (brown not burned); about 20-30 minutes.
5. In a medium bowl, mix the cream cheese, blue cheese, garlic salt and Tabasco.
6. Place the bread slices on a greased cookie sheet and bake for 5-8 minutes until toasted.
7. Take the loin out of the bag, place on the grill, and cook to medium-rare.
8. When the bread is toasted, remove from oven, and spread the cheese mix on each slice evenly.
9. Remove venison loin from grill. Let stand for 8 minutes then slice thinly. Place a slice of venison on the cheese mixture of each bread slice, add some onions on the meat, and repeat.

YIELD: 6-8 servings

SERVE WITH: Favorite beverage of choice.

Lena called the airlines information desk and inquired, "How long does it take to fly from Minneapolis to Fargo? " "Just a minute," said the busy clerk. "Vell, said Lena, "if it has to go dat fast, I tink I'll yust take da bus."

"I tell you the truth, whoever hears my word and believes him who sent me has eternal life and will not be condemned; he has crossed over from death to life."
John 5:24 (NIV)

VENISON *Grill / Sandwich*

VENISON FRENCH DIP SANDWICHES

1 (2-3 lb) whole venison loin, washed well
1 can of Coke
1 large ziplock freezer bag
2 cans beef broth

½ red onion, thinly sliced
2 cups mozzarella cheese
4 hoagie buns, sliced ¾ the way through

1. Wash the venison loin well and lay on paper towels to dry well. Place the loin in the ziplock bag, add the Coke and marinate overnight.
2. In a medium saucepan add the beef broth and onion, simmer for 25 minutes.
3. Preheat grill to medium heat. Take the loin out of the bag and place grill for approximately 8 minutes per side (do not overcook).
4. When loin is done, slice thin and layer the slices inside the hoagie buns. Place sandwiches on cookie sheet and top with cheese.
5. Preheat the oven to 375°. Place the hoagies in the oven and bake until the cheese melts.
6. Pour the beef broth and onion into small bowls and then dip and dunk your hoagies.

YIELD: 4 servings

SERVE WITH: Tator tots and a large chocolate milk shake.

In the middle of the show, Ole stands up and yells at the ventriloquist, "HEY! You've been making too many jokes about us Norwegians! Knock it off ya bum!" The ventriloquist replies, "Take it easy. They're only jokes!" Ole replies, "You idiot, I'm not talking to you. I'm talking to dat little guy sitting on yer knee!"

> *"I heard the voice of the Lord, saying: 'Whom shall I send, and who will go for us?', Then I said, Here am I! Send me.'"*
> Isaiah 6:8 (NIV)

VENISON *Grill / Sandwich*

H&H CHEESE STUFFED VENISON BURGERS (ELK/MOOSE/BEAR)

1 ¼ lbs ground venison
1 Tbsp minced onion
½ tsp black pepper
½ tsp garlic salt
1 egg, beaten

2 pieces string cheese, cut in half
4 eggs
¼ stick butter
8 slices of bacon, cooked
4 hamburger buns

1. In a large mixing bowl, combine ground meat, onion, pepper, salt and beaten egg. Mix well.
2. Take a ¼ cup measuring cup full of burger mix and press flat into a patty. Repeat another 7 times. You should have about 8 flat patties. Now take a piece of string cheese and place on top of one of the patties, then put another patty over the cheese and press the edges of the meat together. Repeat so that you have a total of four cheese stuffed burgers. Place on a grill on medium/low heat, and cook until done.
3. Take a medium-sized frying pan and heat butter over medium heat, then cook eggs over easy and set aside when done.
4. Place the burger on bun, add 2 pieces of bacon, egg, and top of bun.

YIELD: 4 servings

SERVE WITH: French fries and baked beans.

> *Ole* saw a sign on the highway: $200 fine for littering. As he threw a banana peel out of his car window, Ole remarked, "That's fine with me, I could use two hundred dollars."

VENISON *Skillet / Sandwich*

VENISON PATTY MELT

4 slices American cheese
4 slices Swiss cheese
1 ½ lbs ground venison
1 cup onion, sliced

2 Tbsp butter
8 slices rye bread
1 packet of Lipton Onion cup-a-soup mix
1 egg

1. Sauté onions in 2 Tbsp butter until translucent golden and remove from pan.
2. Combine the ground venison, egg, and onion soup mix and mix well and form into four equal size patties.
3. In the same pan over medium heat cook each patty until done.
4. Butter bread on one side. Put buttered side down on hot griddle, layer with 1 slice cheese followed by onions then cooked patty, followed by 1 slice of the other variety of cheese.
5. Butter one side of the other slice of bread and place on top, buttered side out.
6. Fry until bread is crisp, turn over and do the same thing on the other side. Cheese should be well melted.
7. Cut in half when done.

YIELD: 4 servings

SERVE WITH: French fries, for dessert, a banana split.

> "Take my yoke upon you and learn from me, for I am gentle and humble in heart, and you will find rest for your souls."
> Matthew 11:29 (NIV)

Lena once had two chickens. One of them got terribly sick. So she killed the other one to make soup to get the first one well again.

"And the peace of God, which transcends all understanding, will guard your hearts and your minds in Christ Jesus."
Philippians 4:7 (NIV)

VENISON *Grill / Sandwich*

VENISON BURGERS WITH BUFFALO SAUCE

2 lbs ground venison
1 small onion, chopped
1 tsp ground mustard
1 tsp black pepper

1 Tbsp chili sauce
1 tsp minced garlic
6 pieces of jalapeño cheese
6 hamburger buns

Buffalo Sauce: ¼ stick melted butter, 1 Tbsp brown sugar, ¼ cup Red Hot sauce, ¾ cup mayonnaise, ½ cup crumbled blue cheese, ¼ cup chopped celery

1. In a large bowl, combine the ground meat, onion, ground mustard, black pepper, chili sauce and garlic. Mix well, form into 6 equal-size patties.
2. In a medium bowl, combine all the buffalo sauce ingredients and mix very well, then place in the refrigerator.
3. Preheat grill to medium heat. Place the burgers on grill for about 6-10 minutes per side until done. Before removing the patties, spoon on buffalo sauce, place a piece of cheese on each patty and then remove burgers when cheese is melted. Serve on buns.

YIELD: 6 servings

SERVE WITH: Coleslaw and sweet potato fries, then enjoy a root beer float for dessert!

Sven

and Ole buy a mule, but when they get it home, they can't get it into the barn. It just won't go. Sven says, "I know just the problem. He won't fit through the door. His ears are too long." Ole sees that Sven is right, thinks a bit, and then says, "I know what we can do. We should raise the barn by a foot, so he'll fit." Sven asks, "Wouldn't it be easier to dig a ditch for him to walk in?" Ole says, "Sven, don't be such a dummy! It's his ears that are too long, not his legs!"

"Faith means being sure of the things we hope for and knowing that something is real even if we do not see it."
Hebrews 11:1 (NIV)

VENISON Bake / Sandwich

VENISON MEATBALL HOAGIES (ELK/MOOSE/BEAR)

1 ½ lbs ground venison
1 large egg, beaten
1 medium onion, chopped fine
1 tsp minced garlic
1 tsp red pepper flakes
1 tsp black pepper
¼ cup grated parmesan cheese
2 tsp Worcestershire sauce
2 tsp dried oregano
3 cups favorite spaghetti sauce
6 8-inch hoagie buns
6 slices, mozzarella cheese

1. Preheat oven to 450°.
2. In a large mixing bowl, combine the meat, egg, onion, garlic, pepper flakes, pepper, grated cheese, Worcestershire sauce, and oregano. Mix very well. Divide and form 18 meatballs of equal size.
3. Place meatballs on a large baking pan and bake for 12-15 minutes or until done (cut one open a make sure it is cooked all the way through).
4. In a medium saucepan over medium heat, add your favorite spaghetti sauce.
5. Take each hoagie bun and cut ¾ way through, then with your fingers dig out the top part of the bun (not all the way through) to make a boat. Place 3 meatballs in each bun and drizzle some spaghetti sauce over meatballs.
6. Top with a slice of cheese and place sandwiches on a large baking sheet. Bake just until cheese is melted.

YIELD: 6 servings

SERVE WITH: French fries and baked beans. Have a scoop of ice cream for dessert.

Ole and Lars were going ice fishing. It took them three hours just to dig out enough ice to get their boat into the water.

> *"But those who hope in the Lord will renew their strength. They will soar on wings like eagles; they will run and not grow weary, they will walk and not be faint."*
> *Isaiah 40:31(NIV)*

VENISON *Bake / Sandwich*

LIP SMACKIN' CHILI BEAN BURGER

1 packet of Lipton Onion Soup Mix
1 ½ lbs ground meat
½ yellow onion, chopped
1 tsp black pepper
1 egg, beaten
1 (15 oz) can chili beans

1 (15 oz) can black beans, drained
4 dashes Tabasco
1 tsp cumin
½ cup red onion, minced
2 cups shredded cheese

1. In a large mixing bowl, combine the ground meat, egg, yellow onion, pepper, and Lipton soup packet. Mix well.
2. With a 12-place muffin tin, grease all twelve muffin places. Next take ⅔ cup of meat mixture and place inside of the muffin place; press against the bottom and sides creating a bowl shape. Repeat with the other 11 places. Bake in a preheated oven at 375° for 15 minutes. Remove from oven and blot out any grease with a paper towel.
3. While meat is cooking, in a bowl, combine the beans, Tabasco, cumin, and red onion.
4. Take 1 ½ Tbsp of bean mixture and place in each of the meat bowls. Then add as much cheese as you would like over each bean burger. Put back in the oven for 10 minutes at 375°.

YIELD: 6-8 servings

SERVE WITH: Mashed potatoes, gravy and steamed broccoli.

Ole and Lena were always out of ice in their home. They couldn't make it. They could never remember the recipe!

"For I am convinced that neither death nor life, neither angels nor demons, neither the present nor the future, nor any powers."
Romans 8:38 (NIV)

VENISON *Grill / Main Dish*

MITCH'S RIBS

3 racks of baby back ribs
1 cup lime juice
1 ½ cup brown sugar
2 cups tequila
4 cups of rib dry rub
Barbecue sauce on the side (optional)

1. Cut the ribs into "2's" and place them in a very large bowl.
2. Add the lime juice, brown sugar and tequila. Then add water to cover all the ribs and stir well.
3. Place sealable wrap over the bowl and refrigerate overnight.
4. Heat grill to 200°, not any hotter. Place the dry rub in a shallow pan.
5. Take each "2 piece" rib and roll the meaty side in the dry rub and place non-meat side down on the grill; repeat.
6. Cook for 30-40 minutes turning each piece as needed. You will know when they are done when they feel lighter compared to when they were first on the grill.

YIELD: 8 servings

SERVE WITH: Sweet corn, coleslaw and your favorite beverage of choice. For dessert, a slice of banana cream pie.

Lena stepped up to the clerk in the department store and said, "Can I try on that dress in the window?" The clerk responded, "We'd prefer that you try it on in the dressing room."

"You should know that your body is a temple for the Holy Spirit who is in you. You have received the Holy Spirit from God. So you do not belong to yourselves, because you were bought by God for a price. So honor God with your bodies."
1Corinthians 6:19-20 (NIV)

VENISON *Crockpot / Main Dish*

SLOW COOKED VENISON ROAST (ELK/MOOSE/BEAR)

1 medium size roast
1 onion, chopped
3 cups of carrots, chopped
1 packet of Lipton Cup-a-Soup Onion Mix

2 cups of water
1 tsp black pepper
1 tsp garlic salt

1. Wash the roast and place on a layer of 3 paper towels. Place another layer of 3 paper towels over the top and let sit for 10 minutes.
2. Place the roast in the crockpot and add onions, carrots and water. Add pepper, garlic salt and soup mix.
3. Cook on low for 8-10 hours until done.

YIELD: 4-6 servings

SERVE WITH: Baked potato, creamed corn and spinach salad, for desert a slice of apple pie.

Ole bought a farm near Herman, Minnesota. He started out with two windmills, but shortly later took one of them down, he explained, "I figger dere ain't enough vind for TWO of dem."

"Your beauty should come from within you- the beauty of a gentle and quiet spirit that will never be destroyed and is very precious to God."
Peter 3:4 (NIV)

VENISON Skillet / Main Dish

HONEY MUSTARD MOOSE DELIGHT (ANY RED MEAT)

1 ½ lbs of moose cut into bite sized chunks
2 Tbsp olive oil
1 Tbsp black pepper
1 yellow onion, chopped
1 tsp garlic salt
1 package fresh mushrooms, sliced
2 cups fresh spinach
1 cup honey mustard dressing

Marinade: 1 can Coke, 1 Tbsp black pepper, 1 Tbsp olive oil.

1. Add the meat chunks into a large ziplock bag and add the marinade. Marinate overnight.
2. In a large skillet, heat olive oil over medium heat. Add onion and moose chunks, cook until both meat and onions are almost crispy. Add pepper, garlic salt, mushrooms, spinach and cook until mushrooms are soft. Add the honey mustard dressing, mix together.

YIELD: 4-6 servings

SERVE WITH: Wild rice and cranberries, and angel food cake with whipped cream for dessert.

Ole was filling out a questionnaire. To the question regarding Church preference, Ole put down: "Red brick and white trim."

> *"I'm eager to encourage you in your faith, but I also want to be encouraged by yours. In this way, each of us will be a blessing to the other."*
> Romans 1:12 (NIV)

VENISON *Skillet / Main Dish*

SEARED MOZZARELLA VENISON CHOPS (ELK/MOOSE/BEAR)

6 (6-8 oz) venison chops
1 (8 oz) container cream cheese, softened
1 cup shredded mozzarella cheese

¼ cup chopped fresh mushrooms
1 tsp minced garlic
3 Tbsp olive oil

Marinade: 1 can Coke, 1 cup soy sauce, 1 Tbsp black pepper.

1. Wash chops well and lay them on paper towels. Place another layer over the top and let sit for 10 minutes. Place in a large ziplock bag, add the marinade ingredients, and place in refrigerator overnight.
2. In a bowl, combine the cream cheese, mozzarella, mushrooms and garlic.
3. Place a large skillet over medium heat and add olive oil. After the oil is hot, take each chop and place in the skillet, cook on one side until blood and juices start to appear on top side then flip each chop over. Add ¼ cup of the mozzarella mix on the top of each chop. Place a cover over the skillet. Once it melts, the chops should be done (you can add more of the mozzarella mix if you would like). Try not to overcook the chops.

YIELD: 4-6 servings

SERVE WITH: Baked potato, green beans, and garlic toast. I would probably think about a bowl of ice cream for dessert.

Ole and Lena went to the Olympics. While sitting on a bench a lady turned to Ole and said, "Are you a pole vaulter?" Ole said, "No, I'm Norwegian... and my name isn't Valter."

"Give all of your worries to him, because he cares about you."
1 Peter 5:7 (NIV)

VENISON *Bake / Main Dish*

VENISON LASAGNA (ELK/MOOSE/BEAR)

1 ½ lbs ground venison
1 clove garlic, minced
1 Tbsp oregano
1 small onion, chopped
1 (16 oz) can stewed tomatoes
2 (6 oz) cans tomato paste
3 cups cottage cheese

2 eggs, beaten
2 cups ricotta cheese
2 cups cooked spinach
1 package lasagna noodles
2 cups mozzarella cheese
2 cups cheddar cheese

1. Cook lasagna noodles, drain and let cool. Preheat oven to 375°.
2. In a large skillet, add the ground venison and cook over medium heat until browned. Add the onion, garlic, oregano, tomatoes, and tomato paste. Cook for 10-12 minutes; reduce heat.
3. In a large bowl, combine the cottage cheese, ricotta cheese, eggs and spinach. Mix well.
4. Spray a 9x13" pan with non-stick spray. Layer the bottom of the pan with noodles, then spoon on the venison mix and spread evenly. Add another layer of noodles, then the cottage-ricotta cheese mixture and spread evenly. Add another layer of noodles, then add the mozzarella and cheddar cheese.
5. Bake for 45 minutes. Let cool for 15 minutes before cutting and serving.

YIELD: 6-8 servings

SERVE WITH: Warm garlic bread and a Caesar salad. For dessert, enjoy a slice of cheese cake.

Ole and Lena took little Lars to Church for the first time. After the service, they asked him how he liked it, "Vell, da music program was OK, but da commercial vas too long."

"In all the work you are doing, work the best you can. Work as if you were doing it for the Lord, not for people."
Colossians 3:23 (NIV)

VENISON *Pot / Main Dish*

VENISON CHILI (ELK/MOOSE/BEAR)

2 lbs ground venison
2 onions, chopped
2 garlic cloves, minced
1 (14 ½ oz) can diced tomatoes
2 (6 oz) cans green chilies
2 (14 ½ oz) cans chili beans
2 (14 ½ oz) cans kidney beans, drained
1 bottle dark beer
1 (12 oz) can tomato paste

3 (14 ½ oz) cans beef broth
4 Tbsp chili sauce
1 Tbsp cocoa
1 tsp oregano
2 tsp chili powder
1 tsp coriander
1 tsp salt
½ cup brown sugar

1. In a large pot over medium heat, add ground meat, onions, and garlic. Cook until done.
2. Add all remaining ingredients and simmer for 1 hour, stirring occasionally.

YIELD: 6-8 servings

SERVE WITH: Grilled cheese sandwich and a pickle. For dessert, have a bowl of vanilla pudding.

Ole has a slogan at on home on the fridge: "The hurrier I go, the behinder I get."

> *"For I am with you, and no one is going to attack and harm you, because I have many people in this city."*
> Acts 18:10 (NIV)

VENISON *Skillet / Main Dish*

TACO SALAD–VENISON STYLE

2 lbs ground venison
4 cups shredded or chopped lettuce
1 onion, chopped
1 green pepper, chopped
1 (14 oz) can black beans, drained
2 cups Doritos Cool Ranch, crushed
1 (8 oz) can sliced black olives
1 ½ cup sour cream

1 cup Southwestern Dip (vegetable dip)
½ cup Mild Taco Sauce
1 Taco seasoning packet
⅔ cup water
1 cup tomatoes, chopped
2 cups shredded taco cheese blend
1 cup sliced jalapeños (optional)

1. In a large skillet over medium heat, brown the ground venison. Add the onions and green pepper and cook until done.
2. In a LARGE bowl, add the remaining ingredients, add the meat-onion-pepper mixture, and mix very well with salad tongs, and serve.

YIELD: 8-10 servings

SERVE WITH: Spanish rice. For dessert, have fried ice cream.

Lena

passed away and Ole called 911. The 911 operator told Ole that she would send someone out right away. "Where do you live?" asked the operator. Ole replied, "At the end of Eucalyptus Drive." The operator asked, "Can you spell that for me?" There was a long pause and finally Ole said, "How 'bout if I drag her over to Oak Street and you pick her up der?"

"For the wages of sin is death, but the gift of God is eternal life in Christ Jesus our Lord."
Romans 6:23 (NIV)

VENISON *Bake / Main Dish*

SWEDISH MEATBALLS (ELK/MOOSE)

2 eggs
2 lbs ground red meat
½ cup milk
¼ cup minced onion
1 tsp black pepper

1 ½ cups dried bread crumbs
2 (10 oz) cans cream of chicken soup
2 (10 oz) cans cream of mushroom soup
1 (12 oz) can evaporated milk

1. Preheat oven to 350°.
2. In a large bowl, beat egg and mix in the milk. Then add the ground meat, bread crumbs, onion, and black pepper. Shape into 1 ½ inch balls and place on greased baking sheets. Bake for 25-30 minutes.
3. In a medium mixing bowl, combine evaporated milk, cream of mushroom soup and cream of chicken soup.
4. Place the meatballs in a large casserole dish and pour the soup/milk mixture over the meatballs. Bake uncovered for 30 minutes at 375°.

YIELD: 4-6 servings

SERVE WITH: Mashed potatoes, creamed corn and spinach salad. Hot fudge sundae for dessert.

Sven and Ole are roofing a house. Ole picks a nail out of the pan, examines it, and with a "nope" tosses it over his shoulder, he picks up another one does the same thing, picks up a third and after examining it uses it to nail in the shingle. Sven (seeing all of this) exclaims, "Ole! What are you doing, wasting nails like that?" Ole replies, "Well you see, those nails they're pointing towards the house, I can use them. But these nails... they're pointing away from the house, they're useless." "Ole, you IDIOT!!" Sven replies, "Those nails aren't something you just throw away willy nilly... those nails are for the other side of the house."

"But he was pierced for our transgressions, he was crushed for our iniquities; the punishment that brought us peace was upon him, and by his wounds we are healed."
Isaiah 53:5 (NIV)

VENISON *Bake / Main Dish*

MEATLOAF (ELK/MOOSE)

1 ½ lbs ground red meat
1 egg
1 onion, chopped
1 cup milk
1 cup dried bread crumbs

1 tsp chili powder
1 tsp minced garlic
1 cup ketchup
2 Tbsp brown sugar
2 Tbsp ground mustard

1. Preheat oven to 350°.
2. In a large bowl, mix the ground meat, egg, onion, milk, dried bread crumbs, chili powder and garlic.
3. Place in a lightly greased 9x13" baking dish and spread evenly.
4. In a small bowl, combine the ketchup, brown sugar and ground mustard. Mix well. Pour the mixture over the meatloaf and spread evenly.
5. Bake at 350° for 60 minutes.

YIELD: 4-6 servings

SERVE WITH: Mashed potatoes, green beans and a slice of apple pie for dessert.

Ole and Sven were taking a vacation in Sven's new camper. As usual, they'd become lost and were wandering around a strange town trying to find the highway. Sven was just starting down a grade to go under a bridge when he slams on the brakes. Ole said "What you do dat for, Sven?" "Dat sign says "Low Bridge. No Vehicles Over Twelve Feet High. Dis here camper is thirteen feet!" said Sven. Ole says "Look here, Sven, there ain't no cops around. Hit the pedal and go for it!"

> *"That if you confess with your mouth, 'Jesus is Lord,' and believe in your heart that God raised him from the dead, you will be saved."*
> *Romans 10:9 (NIV)*

VENISON *Skillet / Main Dish*

VENISON STIR-FRY (ELK/MOOSE/BEAR)

- 1 lb venison loin
- 1 cup broccoli, chopped
- 1 Tbsp fresh ginger, minced
- 3 garlic cloves, minced
- 1 ½ Tbsp black pepper
- 5 Tbsp olive oil
- 1 green pepper, cut into thin strips
- 1 red pepper, cut into thin strips
- 1 onion, cut into thin slices
- 1 yellow squash, diced
- ¾ cup carrots, chopped
- 2 Tbsp corn starch
- 4 Tbsp soy sauce
- ½ cup honey

1. Wash the venison loin well and place on a layer of 3 paper towels. Place another layer of 3 paper towels over the loin and let stand for 10 minutes. Next, place the loin on a cutting board and cut into thin strips. Place in a large ziplock bag, add 2 Tbsp of olive oil and shake well, then add 1 Tbsp of black pepper and shake again. Let sit for 10 minutes.
2. In a small bowl, combine the cornstarch, honey, and 2 Tbsp soy sauce. Mix until smooth and set aside.
3. In a large deep skillet over medium heat, add 3 Tbsp of olive oil, then add venison, carrots, onion, garlic, ginger root, ½ tsp black pepper and remaining soy sauce. Cook until meat is done. Next add the red and green pepper, broccoli, and squash. Continually stir to mix all ingredients. Place a cover over the skillet, and cook for another 10-14 minutes.
4. Add the honey-soy sauce mixture and let simmer for 3-5 minutes.

YIELD: 4-6 servings

SERVE WITH: Steamed rice and lettuce salad. For dessert, have a slice of pecan pie.

> is so cheap that after his airplane landed safely, he grumbled; "Vell, der gose five dollars down da drain for dat flight insurance!

"Come to me, all you who are weary and burdened, and I will give you rest.
Matthew 11:28 (NIV)"

VENISON *Bake / Main Dish*

VENISON STEW (ELK/MOOSE/BEAR)

2 lbs venison stew meat, cut into 1 inch cubes
1 Tbsp butter
1 Tbsp olive oil
1 lb carrots, sliced
2 medium onions, thinly sliced
2 garlic cloves, minced
1 ½ cups reduced-sodium beef broth

1 bottle (12 oz) ale beer or additional reduced-sodium beef broth
6 medium red potatoes, peeled and cut into 1 in. cubes
1 tsp dried thyme
1 tsp dried rosemary
1 ½ tsp pepper
2 cups ketchup

1. In an oven-proof Dutch oven, brown venison in butter and oil then add the carrots and onions. Cook until tender. Add garlic and cook 1 minute longer. Gradually add broth and beer. Stir in the potatoes, thyme, rosemary, salt, pepper and ketchup.
2. Cover and bake at 325° for 1 ½ to 2 hours or until meat and vegetables are tender, stirring every 30 minutes.

YIELD: 4-6 servings

SERVE WITH: Grilled cheese and a slice of pumpkin pie.

Ole

walks into work, and both of his ears are all bandaged up. The boss says, "What happened to your ears?" Ole says, "Yesterday I vas ironing a shirt ven da phone rang and I accidentally answered da iron." The boss says, "Well, that explains one ear, but what happened to your other ear?" Ole says, "I tried ta call da doctor."

> "Therefore, I urge you, brothers, in view of God's mercy, to offer your bodies as living sacrifices, holy and pleasing to God—this is your spiritual act of worship."
> Romans 12:1 (NIV)

VENISON *Grill / Main Dish*

BLUE CHEESE AND MUSHROOM VENISON LOIN

1 cup soy sauce
¾ cup Worcestershire sauce
1 venison tenderloin (3 ½ to 4 lbs)
3 Tbsp minced garlic
1 Tbsp coarse ground pepper
1 can (10 ½ oz) condensed beef broth, undiluted

Sauce:
½ cup butter, cubed
½ lb sliced fresh mushrooms
2 garlic cloves, minced
¾ cup crumbled blue cheese
1 Tbsp Worcestershire sauce
4 green onions, chopped

1. Wash the venison loin well and place on a layer of 3 paper towels then add another 3 layers of paper towels over the top. Leave for 10-15 minutes.
2. In a large ziplock bag, combine soy sauce, Worcestershire sauce, and beef broth. Add the venison loin; seal bag. Refrigerate for 2 hours, turning occasionally.
3. Drain and discard marinade. Rub the venison with garlic and pepper; place on a preheated medium heat grill. Cook for approximately 4-6 minutes per side (do not overcook).
4. Combine the sauce ingredients in a small sauce pan. Cook for 8-12 minutes over medium heat.
5. Slice the loin and then pour the sauce over the top.

YIELD: 4 servings

SERVE WITH: Steamed asparagus, Caesar salad and cheesecake for dessert.

Ole and Lena went to the hospital so Lena could give birth to their first baby. As Ole waited in the lobby, the doctor came out to inform him that he had some good news and some bad news. "The good news is that you have a normal baby boy. The bad news is that it is a caesarian." Ole started crying: "Vell, I'm glad it is a healthy baby...but I vas kinda hoping it vould be a Norvegian."

"Surely he took up our infirmities and carried our sorrows, yet we considered him stricken by God, smitten by him, and afflicted."
Isaiah 53:4

VENISON *Bake / Main Dish*

VENISON MEXICAN PEPPERS

4 medium green, sweet red, orange and/or yellow peppers
1 egg, beaten
1 cup salsa
1 cup crushed tortilla chips
1 medium onion, chopped
½ cup minced fresh cilantro

½ tsp dried red chili pepper
3 garlic cloves, minced
1 tsp ground cumin
1 lb lean ground venison (90% cooked brown)
½ cup shredded Mexican cheese blend
Sour cream and additional salsa, optional

1. Cut tops off of peppers and remove seeds. In a large bowl, combine the egg, salsa, chips, onion, cilantro, chili, pepper, garlic, and cumin. Crumble cooked beef over salsa mixture and mix well, spoon into peppers.
2. Pour 1 ½ cups water into 8x8" dish. Place peppers in 8x8" dish, cover with aluminum foil, and bake at 375° for 1 hour.
3. Sprinkle peppers with cheese. Serve with sour cream and additional salsa, if desired.

YIELD: 4 servings

SERVE WITH: Vanilla ice cream and fresh raspberries for dessert.

Ole and Lena had been married seven years. Lena was getting worried that Ole might be getting the seven year itch. She thought he was cheating on her. Lena says to Ole, "You never tell me you love me. Is there someone else?" Ole replies, "When ve got married I told you I loved you. If I ever change my mind I'll let ya know."

> "Peter replied, 'Repent and be baptized, every one of you, in the name of Jesus Christ for the forgiveness of your sins. And you will receive the gift of the Holy Spirit.'"
> Acts 2:38 (NIV)

VENISON *Skillet / Main Dish*

VENISON TERIYAKI STIR-FRY

6 venison steaks (approximately 6-8 oz each)
8 spears of asparagus, broken in half
2 red onions, chopped
3 green onions, chopped
Non-stick spray
1 cup teriyaki sauce
1 can Coke

1. Wash the meat well and place on paper towels for 10 minutes. Cut into thin strips and place in a ziplock bag; add a can of Coke and place in refrigerator for at least 2 hours.
2. In a large skillet over medium/high heat, sprayed with the skillet well with non-stick spray add the red onions and cook for 5 minutes, stirring often.
3. Add the asparagus and green onions and cook for 5 minutes.
4. Add the venison strips and cook for 10-15 minutes or until done. Add the teriyaki sauce; stir well and let simmer for another 5 minutes.

YIELD: 4 servings

SERVE WITH: Fried rice. Have some cherry Jell-O with whipped cream for dessert.

Ole came home from a long business trip to find his son riding a new 21 speed mountain bike. "Vere did you get da money for da bike? Dat musta cost $500," he asked. "It was easy, Dad," little Lars replied. "I earned it hiking." "Come on Lars," Ole said. "Tell me da truth." "Dat is da truth Dad!" Lars replied. "Every night you ver gone, Sven would come over to see Mom. He'd give me a $10 bill and tell me ta take a hike!"

"Now to him who is able to do immeasurably more than all we ask or imagine, according to his power that is at work within us."
Ephesians 3:20 (NIV)

VENISON *Skillet / Main Dish*

GROUND VENISON STROGANOFF

1 ½ lbs ground venison
½ cup chopped onion
2 Tbsp butter
2 Tbsp flour
½ tsp salt
¼ tsp pepper

1 garlic clove, minced
1 container of sliced fresh mushrooms
1 can (10 ¾ oz) condensed cream of chicken soup, undiluted
1 cup (8 oz) sour cream

1. In a large skillet, cook ground venison with onion and butter until the venison is no longer pink. Stir in flour, salt, pepper, garlic, and mushrooms. Cook for 10 minutes. Stir in soup. Bring to a boil, stirring constantly.
2. Reduce heat, simmer uncovered for 10 minutes, stirring occasionally. Stir in sour cream. Heat through, but do not boil.
3. Serve over mashed potatoes or egg noodles.

YIELD: 4 servings

SERVE WITH: Steamed asparagus, Caesar salad, and french silk pie for dessert.

Sven and Ole go deer hunting and Ole accidentally shoots Sven. Ole manages to get Sven out of the woods and drives him to the emergency room. After a while, the doctor comes out to Ole in the waiting room. "Doctor, is my friend going to be alright? I drove as fast as I could." "You know, Ole, he might have had a chance if you didn't take the time to prepare him and tie him to the hood of your car."

"For my yoke is easy and my burden is light."
Matthew 11:30 (NIV)

VENISON *Skillet / Main Dish*

CLASSIC VENISON WELLINGTONS

4 venison steaks, dried on a layer of paper towels
¾ tsp salt, divided
½ tsp pepper, divided
2 Tbsp olive oil, divided

1 ¾ cup sliced fresh mushrooms
1 medium onion, chopped
1 package (17.3 oz) frozen puff pastry, thawed
1 egg, beaten

1. Sprinkle steaks lightly with ½ tsp salt and ¼ tsp pepper. In a large skillet, brown the steaks in 1 Tbsp olive oil for 2-3 minutes on each side. Remove from skillet and refrigerate until chilled.
2. In the same skillet, sauté the mushrooms and onion in remaining oil until tender. Stir in remaining salt and pepper, then cool at room temperature.
3. On a lightly floured surface, roll each puff pastry sheet into a 14 x 9 ½ inch rectangle. Cut each into two 7 inch squares. Place a steak in the center of each square; top with mushrooms mixture. Lightly brush pastry edges with water. Bring opposite corners of pastry over steak; pinch seams to seal tightly.
4. Place on a greased 15x10x1 inch baking pan (jelly roll pan). Cut four small slits in the top of pastry. Brush with egg.
5. Bake at 425° for 20-25 minutes or until pastry is golden brown and meat has reached desired doneness.

YIELD: 4 servings

SERVE WITH: Steamed broccoli, Waldorf salad, and cheesecake for dessert.

One day Lena confided to her friend Hilda that she had finally cured her nervous husband, Ole, of his habit of biting his nails. "Good gracious," said Hilda, "How did yew ever dew that?" "It vas really simple," was Lena's reply. "I yust hid his false teeth."

"So God created man in his own image, in the image of God he created him; male and female he created them."
Genesis 1:27 (NIV)

VENISON *Bake / Main Dish*

GROUND VENISON TATER TOT CASSEROLE

2 lbs ground venison
1 Tbsp butter or margarine
1 onion, chopped
1 green pepper, chopped

1 (10.75 oz can) cream of mushroom or cream of chicken soup
1 soup can full of milk
1 (2 lb) package frozen potato tator tots, thawed

1. Preheat oven to 350°. Grease a 9x13" baking dish. In a sauté pan, brown venison over medium heat. Drain off the grease. Remove the venison from the pan and set aside. In the same pan, melt butter. Add onions and green pepper. Sauté over medium heat until softened. Return the venison to the pan, then add soup and milk. Stir to combine and cook for a few minutes until heated through.
2. Line the bottom of the prepared baking dish with half of the tots. Add meat mixture in an even layer. Top with another layer of tots.
3. Bake for 45-60 minutes or until tots are browned and the meat mixture is bubbling.

YIELD: 6-8 servings

SERVE WITH: Green beans, fresh croissants, and chocolate cake for dessert.

Sven and Ole from Minnesota went fishing in Canada and returned with only one fish. "The vay I figger it, dat fish cost us $400", said Sven. "Vell," said Ole, "At dat price it's a good ting ve didn't catch any more."

"Now the Bereans were of more noble character than the Thessalonians, for they received the message with great eagerness and examined the Scriptures every day to see if what Paul said was true."
Acts 17:11 (NIV)

VENISON *Bake / Main Dish*

FIRECRACKER VENISON CASSEROLE

2 lbs ground venison
1 medium onion, chopped
1 can (15 oz) black beans, rinsed and drained
1 to 2 Tbsp chili powder
2 to 3 tsp ground cumin
½ tsp salt

6 flour tortillas (7 inches)
1 can (10 ¾ oz) cream of mushroom soup
1 can (14 ½ oz) diced tomatoes
1 can (4 oz) diced green chilies
1 cup shredded cheddar cheese

1. Cook venison and onions until meat is no longer pink then drain. Add beans, chili powder, cumin and salt.
2. Arrange 2 tortillas on the bottom of a 9x13" greased pan. Pour the venison mixture on top of the tortillas. Arrange the remaining 4 tortillas over the top. Combine soup, tomatoes and green chilies, then pour over tortillas. Sprinkle with cheddar cheese.
3. Bake uncovered at 350° for 25-30 minutes.

YIELD: 4-6 servings

SERVE WITH: Refried beans, Spanish rice, and a scoop of ice cream with warm caramel for dessert.

Sven was going for his morning walk one day when he walked past Ole's house and saw a sign that said "Boat For Sale." This confused Sven because he knew that Ole didn't own a boat, so he finally decided to go in and ask Ole about it. "Hey Ole," said Sven, "I noticed da sign in your yard dat says 'Boat For Sale,' but ya don't even have a boat. All ya have is your old John Deere tractor and combine." Ole replied, "Yup, and they're boat for sale."

"And my God will meet all your needs according to his glorious riches in Christ Jesus."
Philippians 4:19 (NIV)

VENISON *Bake / Main Dish*

THREE-BEAN BAKED BEANS WITH VENISON

½ lb ground venison
5 bacon strips, diced
½ cup onion, chopped
2 cans (16 oz each) pork and beans, undrained
1 can (16 oz) butter beans, rinsed and drained
1 can (16 oz) kidney beans, rinsed and drained
½ cup packed brown sugar

¼ cup ketchup
¼ cup barbecue sauce
2 Tbsp molasses
2 Tbsp yellow mustard
½ tsp chili powder
½ tsp salt

1. In a large skillet or saucepan over medium heat, brown venison, bacon and onion; drain. Add beans. Combine remaining ingredients, and stir into bean mixture.
2. Pour into a greased 2 ½ quart baked dish. Bake, uncovered, at 350° for 1 hour or until beans reach desired thickness.

YIELD: 8 servings

SERVE WITH: French fries and warm corn bread. Chocolate pudding for dessert.

Ole and Lena got married. On their honeymoon trip they were nearing Minneapolis ven Ole put his hand on Lena's knee. Giggling, Lena said,"Ole, you can go farder den dat if you vant to." So Ole drove to Duluth.

"He has showed you, O man, what is good. And what does the LORD require of you? To act justly and to love mercy and to walk humbly with your God."
Micah 6:8 (NIV)

VENISON *Grill / Main Dish*

GRILL BASKET PEPPER VENISON

4 cups venison, cut into 1 inch chunks
1 yellow onion, chopped
1 green pepper, chopped
1 red onion, chopped
1 cup mushrooms, cut in half
1 Tbsp black pepper
⅓ cup olive oil
1 large ziplock bag

1. Combine all the ingredients in the ziplock bag, seal well, and shake to evenly to coat all of the ingredients with the olive oil. Refrigerate overnight.
2. Have your grill going with medium/high heat. Place your grill basket on for 10 minutes. Empty the ziplock bag of ingredients into the grill basket and cook for 15-20 minutes, stirring continuously with a pot holder and wooden spoon.

YIELD: 8 servings

SERVE WITH: Grilled asparagus, hashbrown potatoes, and pumpkin pie for dessert.

Sven and Ole were building a house. Sven was holding a board and Ole was sawing it. All of a sudden, the saw slipped and cut off one of Sven's ears. They both were digging through the sawdust to find it, and Ole picked up an ear. Ole says, " Is this it?" Sven says, "Naw, mine had a pencil behind it."

VENISON *Bake / Main Dish*

VENISON SPAGHETTI CASSEROLE

1 lb ground venison
1 large yellow onion, chopped
4 Ibsp olive oil
2 medium (6 oz) cans of tomato paste with basil and oregano
¼ cup red wine

1 large (29 oz) can tomato sauce
2 tsp black pepper
1 tsp garlic salt
2 cups grated Colby Jack cheese blend
1 lb uncooked penne noodles

1. In a large deep skillet over medium heat, add the olive oil and onion. When onion is clear, add the meat and brown.
2. Add the tomato sauce, tomato paste, red wine, and seasonings. Let simmer for 45 minutes.
3. Cook the penne noodles according to package directions and drain. Combine the noodles and sauce in a large covered casserole. Spread the cheese over the entire top. Cover and bake in a preheated 325° oven for 45 minutes.

YIELD: 4-6 servings

SERVE WITH: Steamed asparagus, Caesar salad, and warm Italian bread. For dessert, a chocolate cupcake with white frosting.

> *Ole* saw this sign on the highway: $100 FINE FOR LTTERING. As he threw the banana peel out his car window, Ole remarked, "That's fine with me…I could use a hundred dollars."

"Let us then approach the throne of grace with confidence, so that we may receive mercy and find grace to help us in our time of need."
Hebrews 4:16 (NIV)

VENISON *Grill / Main Dish*

CORN RELISH VENISON SOFT TACOS

1 ½ lbs venison steak
3 Tbsp Chipotle Tabasco
¼ cup honey
4 Tbsp olive oil
1 tsp black pepper
¼ cup lime juice
12 6-inch corn tortillas

3 limes, cut in half
Relish
6 green onions, chopped
3 cups frozen corn
4 Tbsp olive oil
1 ½ cup cilantro, chopped
1 tsp garlic salt

1. In a large ziplock bag combine the steaks, Chipotle Tabasco, honey, olive oil, pepper and lime juice. Seal and shake; refrigerate overnight.
2. Heat grill to medium heat. Grill steaks for about 5-8 minutes per side (do not overcook, best if pink in middle).
3. While the steaks are cooking, in a large skillet over medium/high heat add the olive oil, onions and then corn. Cook until corn is just turning brown. Place in a medium bowl; add the cilantro and garlic salt and stir well.
4. When steaks are done, slice into thin strips. Prepare each tortilla with steak and a scoop of the corn relish. Squeeze lime juice over the top.

YIELD: 4 servings

SERVE WITH: Spanish rice, refried beans, and for dessert, strawberry shortcake.

> "Delight yourself in the LORD and he will give you the desires of your heart."
> Psalms 37:4 (NIV)

> Ole received minor injuries on the job and was taken the hospital for check up. Typically, there was much paperwork involved. When filling out the blank asking what number to call in an emergency, Ole put down 911.

Other Resources

Ducks Unlimited	www.ducks.org	(800) 45-DUCKS
Pheasants Forever	www.pheasantsforever.org	(651) 773-2000
Minnesota Deer Hunters Association	www.mndeerhunters.com	(800) 450-3337
Whitetails Unlimited, Inc.	www.whitetailsunlimited.com	(800) 274-5471
National Wild Turkey Federation	www.nwtf.org	(800) 843-6983
Ruffed Grouse Society	www.ruffedgrousesociety.org	(800) JOIN-RGS
Rocky Mountain Elk Foundation	www.rmef.org	(800) 225-5335
Minnesota Waterfowler Association	www.mnwaterfowl.com	(952) 761-0320
National Rifle Association	www.nra.org	(703) 267-1000
National Wildlife Federation	www.nwf.org	(800) 843-6983
Izaak Walton League of America	www.iwla.org	(301) 548-0150
Muskies Inc.	www.muskiesinc.org	(888) 710-8286
Trout Unlimited	www.tu.org	(703) 522-0200
Boone and Crocket Club	www.boone-crockett.org	(406) 542-1888
Pope and Young Club	www.pope-young.org	(507) 867-4144
Minnesota DNR	www.dnr.state.mn.us	(888) 646-6367
Quality Deer Management Association	www.qdma.com	(800) 209-DEER
Christian Sportsman's Fellowship	www.christiansportsman.com	(770) 772-6749
Turn In Poachers Hotline		(800) 652-9093
Young Life Great River	www.greatriver.younglife.org	(612) 643-0792
MN Adult & Teen Challenge	www.mntc.org	(612) 373-3366

Mitch Stolba